# COUNT THE STARS THROUGH THE CRACKS

by

Billie Hotaling

**Royal Fireworks Press**
*Unionville, New York*
*Toronto, Ontario*

**FOURTH PRINTING**

---

Copyright © 1998, R Fireworks Publishing Co., Ltd.
All Rights Reserved.

First published in 1992 by KAV Books, Inc.

Royal Fireworks Press
First Avenue, PO Box 399
Unionville, NY 10988-0399
(914) 726-4444
FAX: (914) 726-3824
email: rfpress@frontiernet.net

Royal Fireworks Press
78 Biddeford St
Downsview, Ontario
M3H 1K4 Canada
FAX: (416) 433-3010

ISBN: 0-89824-988-0

Printed in the United States of America on acid-free, recycled paper using soy-based inks by the Royal Fireworks Printing Company of Unionville New York.

# CHAPTER ONE

## Escape

"Susu, get up."

One long braid hanging over her bed in the darkness scratched against the quilt. Hushed fear in her Momma's voice drove clean to the bone. Susu hunched further into the hollow her body made in the dry, sweet grass mattress.

"Get up," she heard again, softer, more urgent.

The cabin door swung open on leather hinges, gloom beyond outlining Jute before he ducked in and shut the door behind him. His strong arms shook Susu impatiently as he shoved the rough cloth dress under her nose. His harsh gesture left no time for doubt. She groped for the neck hole, stuck her head through, searching around for the sleeves later.

"Take this," he hissed, tossing a bundle in her direction. It slid off the bed landing on her foot with a muffled rattle. As Susu stooped to pick it up with both arms, Jute prodded her from behind.

"We're scampin," he whispered, his lips breathing hot against her ear. "Now!"

She knew it. She'd known it all along and was afraid. She knew it from the moaning nights, the fear in her Momma's voice, Jute and the way he was acting. A tight pain clutched her, remembering how it had been these last days with Poppa gone.

All the women jumbling out there every night on the steps. Singing songs like, "No More Sickness, No More Sorrow, When I Lay My Burden Down." But Momma's voice came through the rest moaning, sobbing; the holler of it never left Susu's throat, aching with the silent words.

Poppa's gone, gone, gone where? She never dared to ask. Last night Susu fell asleep as she always had, the tick stuffed with dry grass smelling good, the spaces between the logs wide, the bunks built close enough that she could count the stars through the cracks. She'd wondered, would they really ever go? Out somewhere in the night to "Freedom's Heavenly Shore." Now it had come. She wanted to crawl back into the hollow of the bed she knew.

She stumbled out of the cabin following Jute up there loping like a cat with his slit eyes, black skin shining, and his straight-line mouth set.

Jute made them go. "Moan, momma, moan," he'd said. "If we don't leave now, we're like to get sold along side of Poppa, and you to care for that new house baby instead of yourn that's dead." Jute made them go. Remembering his voice, Susu shivered cold and naked under her dress. It's cold and wet, should have been asleeping she thought. Her heart was tight, making it hard to breathe. She padded on, her bare feet feeling for the ridges in the path down to the river. She shifted the heavy bundle to rest on her hip. Too late to go back now; they were on their way.

Jute, Susu, and Momma skirted the edges of the wood between the tangled forest and the smooth wet lawn, the black mass of the big house towering above them, sitting high and mighty above the river. Terraced gardens stepped down the broad tobacco fields before they reached the wandering brackish shore. The Saint Mary's River, more like an inlet of the Chesapeake than a river here, so wide in places you can hardly see across, an island sitting off shore like a turtle poised to snap.

Susu heard a new sound, the slap, slap of water against the side of a boat, where no boat should have been.

"Hisst, watch it." Jute's voice was soft, curling around the words like a snake on a limb.

Momma was behind her, no moaning now, no words, nothing, padding along. Jute waded in and held the boat, a skiff pulled up on the rocky beach.

"Get in, Susu," he said grabbing her arms to steady her as she held back.

Scrabbling in, another hand reached out to take the bundle, to help her forward. Susu almost fell back into the water. It was a white hand. No moon, but she could clearly see it stretched out to her, pale against a dark sleeve, reaching out for her.

"Come on, girl," a man's voice said. "Up here in the fore and squat down."

A hard pull and she was in her place, down as low as she could get, clutching the bundle to her chest. Momma sat down beside her. Jute pushed off and the boat floated free.

The man in the middle pulled at the oars. Pull-turn-drip the repeated rhythm almost putting her to sleep. She wasn't so cold now, her skirt pulled over her doubled knees she huddled down beside her Momma.

Jute sat aft, high up on the gunwales of the oyster boat, watching, listening, every sense alive, keen, tuned to the night. His narrowed eyes patrolled the bank on his right. Were all the dark shapes rooted there or did they creep closer to the shore? His ears singled out the sleepy call of the night birds across the water, the measured dip of the oar, pearled drips of water after each slice.

Excitement dried his throat. He'd brought them there, he thought. His whispered talk with the men in the tobacco fields after Poppa was sold, with Mr. Willett's field hands, when they brought fodder for the animals from Mulberry Fields upriver. Jute had heard as long ago as

3

last summer that folks were slipping through up North, helped by Willett. But none had dared leave from his place; he'd be the first! Glen Mary wasn't bad. Families lived together. After baking days, knee deep in tobacco, there was food, singing, and sleep. But old Miss was changing things now that the master was dead. Some men gone, families split. Fingers pointed, no one knew who would be next, or where they went.

Jute sifted the rumors and waited. Willett owned Mulberry Fields. He was a Quaker who kept his own slaves as a shield while he helped other folks get away. People came from Virginia, far away as Georgia even. Why Willett did it Jute couldn't figure. He didn't know how they made contact, and he listened a long time before asking. Now it was too late to wonder if it was right for them. Canada was just a name, but getting away was real.

Jute fingered the handle of the knife stuck in his hemp belt stolen from the pig house yesterday. Killing time was way back. It hadn't been hard to pry open a high window and drop down inside the stone slaughter house. All the scrubbed tools gleaming in their slots. The trough for the dripping blood, everything ready for the next time a pig was stuck. He'd chosen a knife sharp enough to skin the hide.

No turning back now he thought. He'd slit each dog's throat holding the head between his knees stroking the long silky ears. They died without a gurgle. Not part of Mr. Willett's plan, his own. No barking dogs to wake the family, none to sniff their trail down to the river. The boat moved on. Jute looked up at Mr. Willett. Funny kind of white man rowing the boat and letting him sit there wondering.

The plan had been set for a week. Passed on by Willett's head man. "Carry only what you can," he'd said.

"Bring everything warm to wear, a cup, and spoon. Wait for the first night without a moon. Wait down by the river about an hour after the last light in the big house is out."

Mr. Willett leaned forward in the boat. "Watch for the mooring at our place," he said. "It's far out in the river painted white."

Lord help them, he thought, as he always did. Lord help them get through to freedom. This family should stay together. He'd never seen them before but he'd heard enough to make up his mind to help. A grieving mother, her own baby lost, her dress barely covering her swelling breasts meant to suckle the youngest Fahnstalk child. Grieving for a husband torn away. He'd singled her out yesterday when he talked to the overseer Jenkins about the wells. She'd walked past him with a basket of soiled linen from the house, never glancing up, her eyes burning with sorrow. She had high cheek bones and one long swinging braid. Her bronze skin burnished. Some Indian blood there he'd thought. The little girl, no more than ten, scared eyes following every move. She'd almost jumped out when helped into the boat. Clutching her knobby knees now and a bundle of woolen stuff too large for her to carry, he could make out her hair, done up in many little braids, each tied with a colorful strip of cloth. Someone cared. He sighed aloud.

But it was the boy who interested Mr. Willett the most. The boy that he had not been able to turn away. Even with suspicions darkening in the county, and townfolk whispering that the Quakers held their own meetings and thought different on this slavery issue. Soon they'd catch on to what he was doing and stop him any way they could. The boy couldn't be more than fifteen, seventeen maybe, smoldering for a father sold without warning, smoldering with a hate that wouldn't let it happen to the rest of them.

Ross Willett had no arrangements made this run. Hide them in the pent till a vessel could be trusted or a wagon going overland through Pennsylvania. Didn't usually do things without a plan but there'd been no time. Mrs. Fahnstalk was closing up most of the tobacco fields, selling the men for the cash. He didn't know the reason. So here he was with an ailing woman, a scared child, and a half-grown man with the fire of the devil within him and steel born of hate. Could they get through?

\* \* \*

"I see it," said Jute, pointing to the dock slightly higher than the surrounding water.

"Yes," answered Ross. "But we'll land just short of it on the inlet. No sand there, brush down to the water. Climb over that and there'll be no footprints. Don't worry about dogs. They've had bread soaked in brandy, should sleep till noon. I don't want my people to see thee. Less folks know you're here the less chance the patrollers will have to catch thee. Mrs. Willett will take care of thee at night. No one else sleeps in the house."

The boat landed with a soft thud against a driftwood log, its branches reaching toward the sky. Susu scrambled out first, her bare feet surefooted on the smooth warm wood. Mulberry Fields was close to the water and down low, its cabins off far to the left in a small cluster of pines. The only sounds were the whirring katydids in the June night. As the little band reached the low white house, a wide wooden door opened soundlessly inward. Ross crossed the broad porch, raised only a foot above the ground. Jute, Susu, and Momma followed, silent still, pressing against each other in the wide hall.

Susu felt the thick colorful rugs beneath her toes. She stared at the women holding a silver candlestick steady and high. The door closed as suddenly as it had opened.

"Welcome. May the way be safe for thee here," Mrs. Willett said softly. Leading the way, she motioned for them to follow over the many carpets and a stretch of cool polished wood into a long room filled with dark furniture. Mrs. Willett stooped next to the large fireplace. She pulled a small brass ring hidden in the wall next to the fire tongs and brush leaning against the stone. A small door opened out, almost triangular in shape, not disturbing the pink lustre plates leaning on the plate rack above it. One by one they followed the beckoning candle. Only Susu did not need to stoop to enter. Inside, the walls next to the chimney were tall, reaching to the second story with a small half-moon window on the outside way up near the top. The room was long and narrow, bricked on all sides. In the winter the pent helped heat the whole house, holding the warm air trapped like an oven. Another one on the far side of the house backed on the other side of the giant chimney. Some hooks, used to dry food, held wraps for cold weather. Pallets lay on the floor with quilts folded at the bottom of each. A chamber pot stood in the corner and on a shelf a white pitcher. This room had been used to hide people before.

"Thee will be warm here in the pent. Be very quiet. I'll bring some food later," Mrs. Willett added as she left, closing the odd shaped door.

Momma sat on a pallet rocking back and forth, back and forth, no moaning now, she thought, remembering Jute's words. She couldn't even moan. Tears slid down her face in the dark. No one to call her "Mary" now. No one to turn to her in the night. If Poppa should get back, she'd be gone. Where? Jute and Susu gone with her.

Canada was a never place. People talking. She never heard of no one making it. They left. No one ever saw them again.

Susu was curled up on a quilt already asleep still clutching the bundle. Momma reached her hand out to pat her, but she was too far away.

Jute stretched out, eyes glinting from the faint light of the high window. Could she make it, for him Momma wondered? He wanted it so. To be free. Wherever he went she'd have to go, too. She fell asleep with no clear picture in her mind of where she was headed, or even the place behind. Just a hot head and a crying feeling. No one would call her Mary anymore.

# CHAPTER TWO

## In the Pent

It was morning when the door opened again, but the sunlight angling from the high window did not quite reach the floor. A twilight air remained forever trapped within the pent.

"Thee did not eat last night," said Mrs. Willett, placing an oval tray of food on the shelf.

Rice, greens, and biscuits, with a pitcher of milk, spoons, and mugs.

Susu looked at the lavender-gray skirt as Mrs. Willett brushed past the quilt where she was sitting. Suddenly Mrs. Willett swooped down, taking Susu's narrow chin in her cupped hand. Susu flinched at the unexpected touch. The smooth face so close to her own, light brown hair caught back in a net, the circle of a gold brooch on the small, round collar.

"People will come today to ask about thee," said Mrs. Willett, giving Susu's chin a little shake. "Does thee understand? There must be no noise. It is dangerous for us all. Thee would be beaten very much back home," she add gently.

"Yes, ma'am," Susu breathed, without a sound—she knew! No need to tell her to be quiet if men came asking questions.

Mrs. Willett left.

Jute was sitting on the edge of the pallet. A coiled spring. He didn't move toward the dishes.

Momma rose, padding between them with the food and mugs of milk.

Trying not to clink her spoon against the plate, Susu finished the food her Momma brought her. She licked her plate and wiped it with her skirt. Shiny white with blue flowers, shiny white. She knew it would break if she dropped it on the brick floor of the pent.

Susu had never eaten off a plate before; her bowl at home was made of wood. It could shine too when she wiped it clean. Her bowl was just as good for food, even held soup and gruel. Susu held the pretty plate cool against her cheek, then traced the pale blue flowers with the tip of one finger, traced the wreath till she got back to the first flower and started over again.

Momma was rocking on her quilt, back and forth, back and forth, no moaning now. Susu moved next to her, rocking as Momma rocked, close, touching, careful not to drop her plate. Jute ranged up and down the narrow room, making a pattern with his feet, same number of steps up, over, and back each time. Seemed like the whole day went by, but the light hadn't changed much in the high window.

Jute was ready for them when they knocked. Harsh rattle of metal knocker at the front door, muffled only by the distance and the partition in between. Stamping feet, loud voices, but no dogs. Jute looked around. Momma stopped rocking. Susu still clutched her like they froze there.

"Come in and sit a spell," he heard a man's voice saying, finally able to hear the words.

"Thee must be tired from all that tramping in the woods."

"You don't think the same as we do on this secession," a fighting voice began.

Jenkin's voice: The overseer! Right on the other side of that door.

Susu and Momma heard it too and recognized it.

Jute could tell.

Seemed like Jenkins could hear them breathing here on the far side of the wall.

"Thee must believe what God has told thee right," said Ross Willett quietly. "Let Nora bring some tea."

"We'll sit a spell," said Jenkins grudgingly.

"Good," said a third man, "that holly tore clear through my skin. Don't believe we've met ma'am. I'm Christie, second in command to Jenkins here, back at Glen Mary."

"Thee could use some salve," said Willett, "Nora!"

"Never mind, I've had worse treks out hunting, but then we had dogs."

"Thee has no dogs?" asked Ross.

"Killed," said Jenkins. "Throats slit, every one, even the bitch about to litter."

"No!" breathed Ross in genuine surprise and distate.

"That's a murdering devil, that Jute. Don't know that I would like to catch up with him alone. Young as he is, you'd best be careful.

"Half Indian, ain't he?" asked the third man.

"Somethin' like that, Christie. Mixed with darky," answered Jenkins. "The very worst kind; got the bad points of each. I think the boats will catch up with them. No signs they went overland."

"Boats?" asked Ross.

"The men split up," said Jenkins. "All we could muster. Half went down river, half up. We came through the woods to see if you'd heard anything. If you weren't too busy drowning it out with one of those everlasting meetings of yours."

"Our meetings are silent," Ross answered coldly. "We would have heard anything strange."

The voices grew more muffled as the men left the drawing room.

"How many did thee say escaped, and what time was it?" asked Ross at the door. "Don't hold with those who don't agree," growled Mr. Jenkins. "Meddlers can go up North and leave Maryland for those of us who knows where we belong—we're South!"

"Thee must believe what God has told thee right," Ross said again.

"Mind if Christie here stays with you a few days to keep an eye on the place? They could show up here yet. You've such a good vantage point of the river from your porch being close and all," Jenkins's voice oiled on as if the thought was new.

"We'd be pleasured to have thee, Mr. Christie. Thee will be returning with thy trappings?"

"Kind of you," muttered Christie.

"Why not borrow horses?" pressed Ross.

"We'll walk back by the road," said Jenkins.

"I'll be back," said Mr. Christie, "soon." A threat or a promise?

Their footsteps crunched the gravel walk away from the shore.

Susu's hands were stiff. She'd made a mark on Momma's arm.

Jute didn't move, still listening for footsteps no longer heard.

The door opened.

"Thee must leave. It's not safe here now. Mr. Christie will soon be back," Mr. Willett said gently.

"We have a meeting every night at dusk. All my workers are there. When you hear the bell toll, head for the island offshore. There is a dugout shelter on it underground. It's been used before and should protect you till they give up and look for you farther away."

"No fires. Boats will be patrolling the river. Thee will be cared for as here. My men will reach you when it's safe to move on. You can walk to the island when the bell tolls. At low tide there's a sand bar on this side all the way. It won't be deep, even for her."

Willett pointed toward Susu, but only talked to Jute.

"Understand?" he said.

Jute nodded.

## CHAPTER THREE

## Tippity Whitchity Island

Susu huddled into herself, counting the bell tolls.

Old Sarah had taught her to count sorting linen in the laundry shed back home. Heavy caldrons bubbled over hot coals as they counted sheets and cases from the big house. Susu's back ached with remembered hours of stirring the steamy clothes, pulling them out to dip into the cold water kettles she had filled with bucket after bucket from the well.

"Four, five, six," she counted to herself.

"Come," said Jute, wrenching her shoulder in his wiry hand.

"Here," the bundle was again thrust into her arms.

She stumbled through the doors of the pent. Her Momma, already out, crossed the big room, bare feet padding on the flowery carpet.

Jute opened the front door a crack, peering down to the shore before stepping softly out, on cat-steps unheard even by Susu's straining ears.

Last, she closed the door behind her. The latch clicked softly and all was quiet. The day was warm and almost light still. Scary, coming out of the big house door into the day like this! Nobody around who belonged here to lead them away.

The shore was sandy in front of Mulberry Fields.

"Wait," said Jute, to Momma about to cross the beach.

"We don't need no footprints here. Lie down," he whispered.

Susu and Momma squatted low, watching Jute hunt over the shore. He came back with a long plank.

"Do what I do," he said, crossing the plank to the water beyond.  Susu went next.  She left her bundle on the grassy slope as she inched along the narrow splintered board, careful not to step on the beach.  Momma crossed with long sure strides.  Jute returned for the bundle, running along the plank the last time.  With bounding steps he splashed into the water, shoving the plank free, it drifted downstream.

Still no one in sight!  The big house, cabins, cook house, and all deserted.  Mr. Willett was sure having a long meeting tonight.

Cold water swirled around Susu's ankles as she waded over the oyster shells.  Soon it reached her dress.  Momma, the bundle now on her head, stretched out hard for her hand.  Momma must be thinking what she was thinking. 'Bout the island and how nobody ever went there!

Snake Island, the black folks called it.

Susu'd heard there were so many snakes you couldn't put your foot down without stepping on one.  An' haunts of all the people who'd been bit, just walking around with sticks to beat 'em with.

Momma must've been thinking that, too.  But she walked straight and tall, one hand holding the bundle on her head, and the other holding Susu, strong against the pull of the water now above her waist.  Susu lost touch with the bottom sometimes, but the water never came above her chin.  She feared plenty.  She pulled herself dripping, shivering, on to the stony bank opposite, peering about for snakes.

Jute looked behind again.  No one following! Momma wrung the water out of her skirt.  Jute waved an arm from behind the cover of some brush, and they ducked in beside him.

Momma unwrapped the bundle, handing Susu her other dress and winter shawl. She skinned off her wet clothes and spread them on the brambles to dry as Momma did.

Can't see any snakes, she thought.

Susu and Momma sat with their backs against the stone waiting for Jute to finish poking around the island. Didn't take him long; the whole island was smaller than the tobacco fields back home.

Jute had heard snake tales, too. He carried a big stick and beat the branches aside as he searched for the shelter. "Look for a boulder leaning against a dead tree," Mr. Willett'd said. "At the foot of the tree is a green vine. Pull it and a trap door covered with sod will lift up. Leave no footprints on the island, especially around the entrance of the dugout!"

Jute swung his stick at the tangled bushes, keeping an eye on the overgrown path for any sign of snakes, walking to one side where the weeds were thick.

He remembered Mr. Willett's description.

"Old hideout from Indians we fixed up recently. Plenty of air; there's holes pulled up by the roots of the dead trees. Make no fire. There's food in the shelter."

Everything fixed for them again! Jute wondered why he felt so mean. This had been his plan, but so far only the starting out and killing the dogs was his own idea. Willett took over everything else. White boss men as always.

He found the rock when his stick cracked into something hard, instead of bushes. It took a while to spot the vine looped about in a knot. He yanked. A door lifted up. By his feet was a gaping cellar hole dug into the red dirt under a dead tree.

Jute left the door open and went back for the others. Snatching up wet clothes, cups, and mugs from the scattered bundle, Jute led them to the cave, covering all their tracks with leaves.

"Snakes!" said Momma, holding back as Jute climbed into the cave.

"Warn't none. I searched," said Jute.

But he hit all the sides again with his stick, poking into every crack while the open trap door still let in some light from the darkening sky. His stick caught the food tin with a resounding crack. Stiffened, listening sharp a minute, they waited. There was no answering sound.

Jute sprang down into the shelter and lifted Susu beside him. Momma clambered in and Jute pulled the vine to shut the trap door behind them. Susu smelled moldering fern and damp earth. She crouched inside the cave. Momma could almost stand. She opened the tin and handed each of them a handful of dried apples, followed by two hard biscuits. Hard, but not moldy. They tasted good as Susu crunched her evening meal. If only she had some of the good, clear water from the well back home.

"Can't look for water tonight," Jute warned, like he knew what she was thinking. "Those men might be following close. Stay put while we're safe hid."

Susu settled down again. She kept looking at the gray light coming in from the holes above. Only place for snakes to get in! I'll seek out them holes all night, she figured, and staring hard at the dirt with its dark and light patches above her, Susu fell asleep.

Hollowed out dirt all around him, Jute was sharpening a peeled stick with the stolen knife, when the hullabaloo started on the river.

One sharp call echoed by another boat downstream.

Shaking Susu and Momma awake, he flung the arrow-shaped stick against the cave wall where it quivered, its peeled sides showing white against the blood red dirt.

"Patrollers," he said. "Don't sneeze nor nothing."

"On the island?" asked Momma fearfully.

"Not yet." Jute's answer was hushed, waiting.

Susu sat up between them. She remembered the snakes and continued her watch above. Snakes and men hunting them down like jack rabbits. What was the matter with home anyway? Poppa had gone, but he wasn't here neither. Not even water to drink!

She sat up close to Momma, touching Jute, too. He backed off as if he couldn't listen as well with her leaning on him. Well, if he was going to be prickled she wouldn't get near him no matter how scared she was.

Twice more men called over the water. The last time the words— "Search the island?" pierced the night.

"Not yet, might just as well," streamed back on the wind.

No more words.

Great crashing sounds converged upon the center of the island, and went out again like the spokes of a wheel.

Shouting men, stumbling through the moon-lit undergrowth, thrashing the bushes with their clubs. Twice, thundering boots jarred close to the cave, sending clods of dirt down into faces upturned with fright.

Able to stand it no longer, Susu hid her head in Momma's lap. Momma's hands smoothed over her head, again and again, feeling good, almost steady.

Were the men going to camp there and never leave?

Susu stifled a scream, aching in her throat to get out, to be free, to run splashing into the water, away from the island and its trapped hiding place. Her eyes were hot and tired from staring at the dark, her body cramped forever.

At last the men moved off. Their crashing through the tangled growth no longer jarred the ground above. Small pebbles stopped raining from the ceiling of the cave.

A shot rang out, two, three, before they heard scraping boat noises and the clanking of oars in rusty oarlocks.

"Snakes!" whispered Jute.

Susu's back ached. She stood up to stretch, but Jute's strong arm snatched her back again. Her relief came out in angry thoughts about Jute.

Boss man! That's what he thought he was. Boss Man! Nothing to drink in this place. Even white men left.

No more sounds sifted into the cave. Jute listened all night. Wild ducks flew back to shelter in reedy coves on the far side of the island.

Feeling safer, Jute lifted the trap door at dawn. They needed water! He fetched the kettle brought in the bundle from home. The spring was only a bubbling spot near mossy rocks.

Tracks of small animals ringed the mud around it. Scooping it deeper with both hands, Jute was able to press his kettle down low enough to fill with cold water.

Momma was praying when he returned. Eyes turned up to the opened door, and sky beyond. Her lips moved soundlessly. Finished, she leaned back, looking sick and tired. Since the baby died, her eyes were flat, her high cheeks hollow. Something missing—hope maybe.

"Leave me play," begged Susu. "The men are gone. Leave me run free. My legs get to ache from sitting so long."

Jute angered fast. Looking at him like he was the enemy, keeping her from running free! Susu always acted like he was keeping her from something, 'stead of leading her to the promised land.

"Go where you like," he muttered.

"Here," he said, pushing the kettle of spring water over to her as she climbed out. She guzzled the icy drink trying to make it last.

Susu was soon playing nearby. Collecting red berries, bending twigs into doll-folk, braiding vines for their head, and neck. Like she was back home and didn't know or care about Canada or freedom.

Momma rocked her as she had in the pent, and in the cabin back home.

Jute felt caged and alone. Ready to break out on his own away from Willett's plans, and these two holding him back. Turning with a sigh, he knew he'd never leave them. One reason for going was to keep the family whole. From behind the bushes he scanned the shore over and over, looking for some sign from Mulberry Fields. Sometimes he could make out figures near the house. Could be Mr. Christy, or even Jenkins back again. He daren't wave or holler. Get stove back home that way sure. He stretched his long legs, aching to move, or put more miles between him and Glen Mary. He was trapped by the island.

Three times it got light and dark again. After days of waiting, Jute wanted to tear out and swim for shore. Each night he strained for sounds of Mr. Willett's return. He'd left them there! Forgotten! They'd rot or starve when the food ran out. Shouldn't have put his trust in a white man.

On the fourth night Susu brought a stick she had frayed and handed it to Momma. Squatting down in front of her as she used to in the cabin door at home, she began untying the knotted cloth that bound her braids. Momma's hands, sure and steady, raked through her tangled hair. The stick brushed over and over. Momma didn't hurt. Again and again the brushing sound mixed with the rustling of almost-night in the wood.

The braids were nearly finished. Only a few more bright, narrow strips to be tied, when a soft halloo curled through the thicket.

Jute glanced up at the open trap door, opened all the time now, as they crouched within. His long arm flashed up and pulled the twisted vine. The door thudded shut. Waiting inside, Momma's hands finished the job, surely in the dark as in the day. A quickening of her fingers the only sign she had heard.

They felt footsteps approach above.

"Jute, Jute, you there?" a low voice called, close beyond the closed door.

Jute slowly raised the warm planks covered with moss and leaves.

Ross Willett bent by the opening.

"Bring all thy belongings, " he said.

His firm hand guided Momma's.

"Follow me, Mary," he said gently.

Ross noticed her answering smile. The first he's seen. All through the time spent in the room behind the fireplace at Mulberry Fields, her dark eyes glittered as if filled with tears that never spilled over. Maybe they had a chance, he thought. She leaned heavily on him as if weak from the time spent in the cave. Her breathing came hard with a wheeze he'd not noticed before. No time for Nora to mix a remedy.

Jute lifted Susu out for the last time. She left her store of pebbles and berries, but clutching a twig doll and the brush, ran to keep up with the others, dodging branches flung back in her face.

Suddenly she stopped, gasping with fright. There on the path before her lay a big black snake. The first she'd seen on the island except the dead one the patrollers had shot down near the shore. The others, almost out of sight, headed through the bushes for the shore. The snake, coiled, looked at her, its mouth opening and closing over a darting tongue. Susu gathered up her skirts, high above her knees, and clutching them to her side she gave a bounding leap over the snake, steadying herself as she landed beyond it.

Panting, without looking back, she pushed herself harder to catch up. She ran along, heedless of the brambles tearing her bare skin, pulling at her arms and legs. She caught up with them at last, as they reached a beached skiff.

"We needst hurry to meet that barge," said Ross Willett.

Jute followed the pointing finger, seeing for the first time a shape upriver. Dusk drawing about them shielded the form and distance of the vessel.

"We must hurry," Ross repeated. "He shan't tarry there long."

Jute sat beside Willett on this trip, on the wide middle seat of the oyster boat. Momma and Susu huddled aft, the bundle drawn up between them.

Willett pulled hard toward the darkening shape, both hands on one oar. Jute did the same on the other, his young muscles straining against the wood. He'd make the boat turn leeward he thought. He was stronger than any white man! But the boat stayed steady on its course.

It was harder to see the barge now, only the dark banks stood out solid against wavering water as the skiff pulled on.

Susu wasn't angry at Jute any more. Seemed she's always travelled like this, without knowing where she was going, or where they'd stay that night. She missed the singing back home, Poppa, and her bunk with the sweet grass tick. But she moved on, pulled by the wonder of what came next.

The barge loomed up suddenly, its bulk high above their small craft. Folks must eat on a ship that big, Susu thought as they slid along side, stopping with a jolt when Mr. Willett caught the rope hanging over the side.

Momma looked at the barge, its planks roughened and gray from long use on the river. She saw the square sail lowered. Now the boat was anchored.

Jute got them there she thought, and all these men helping him, so they wouldn't be sold like Joss, no one knew where. Maybe there was a promised land.

## CHAPTER FOUR

## The Barge

A rope ladder lowered down to the skiff danced in the small night breeze. Mr. Willett held it steady as Momma and Susu climbed to the top and stepped aboard the narrow deck. No one was in sight. As if abandoned there, the barge rocked gently in the ebb of St. Mary's tidewater, its square sail lowered.

"The rivermen know about thee," Mr. Willett said to Jute as they stood for a moment unsteadily in the bobbing oyster boat.

"Stay aboard till the bend before Alexandria. The town lights should show up ahead before you disembark. The men know the farm, my cousin James's place. He'll be expecting the tobacco shipment and thee."

Mr. Willett seemed about to push off with his windward oar. "Follow closely what my cousin tells thee to do," he said, pressing a small box into Jute's hand. "Here, thee may have need of these."

Jute stooped for the bundle braced against his feet in the gunwales of the boat. As he swung it up with one hand, he dropped the small tin box Mr. Willett had given him inside its folds without looking at it. He skinned up the ladder. The words he had for this man caught in this throat.

Willett had everything his way, planning where they stopped and when—even planning for the trip ahead. Some of it was good. He was shut of Glen Mary. He'd never go back there again, never. That thought alone was almost worth taking orders from white men he didn't really know.

Silently Jute turned. Still holding the top rung, he waved the bundle at Ross Willett pulling toward the shore. Ross nodded. Night swelled around him, water, sky and skiff blotting together.

Jute glanced at the barge as he stepped over the side. Many river barges tied up to Glen Mary's dock; he'd even loaded some when they were short of hands. He knew they left St. Mary's River and rounded Piney Point before heading up the Potomac as far as Washington.

"There's space below the cupboard shelf for you folks," said a large man appearing in the doorway of the small fore cabin, almost filling the door frame with his bulk. He wiped his seamy red face with the back of his sleeve. Graying whiskers curled around a grimed captain's hat, jammed on his head. His eyes almost disappeared when he smiled unexpectedly down at Susu, crouched shivering on the deck.

"I'm Captain Moore," he added more gently just to her. He gave Jute a nudge toward the open hatch. A fixed ladder on its side pitched down to the black hold below. Momma and Susu hung back, the rolling boat beneath their feet hard to stand up to. Water from below them prodded the anchored barge.

Jute jerking his head for them to follow, disappeared down the ladder. With lurching steps Momma and Susu joined him.

The familiar smell of dried tobacco filled the cupboard shelf between the decks. Bales piled unevenly with spaces in between made a good resting spot. Two deck hands lounging there nodded toward the bow.

Captain Moore called down the open hatch, "Just settle anywhere a'fore cabin and stay out of sight when this lighter stops."

Susu's eyes could soon pick out shapes in the gloom of the hold. She pushed two bales together for her bed. No one stopped her. The men near the hatch-opening glanced at Jute as he sat down. She shoved more bales about, upending some with effort, until she'd made herself a crib of warm, sweet, dry tobacco, smelling like the drying sheds back home. She hitched her skirt about her shoulders as she lay curled up listening. Men's voices rumbled from the dark as they had ranged from the cabin stoop, accompanied now by the steady slap of water near her head.

Momma made her bed behind high piled bales in the bow, out of sight. She slipped back there without a word to Susu or to Jute. She lay looking up into the dark, her face hot. She didn't even wipe the trickling sweat, an almost forgotten song in her mind kept rhythm with the water's swell. "Chariot carrying me home."

Jute sat on the edge of a bale near the lounging men, glad to see some dark folks down here.

"We're supposed to call you the shipment," said one hand, grinning at Jute, "What were you called back on the home place?"

He was tall and black with a jagged tear across his ear as if an earring had been yanked out long ago. A kerchief of red figured stuff was tied around his throat above a bare and glistening chest.

"Jute," said Jute.

The other man slouched against the side of the boat, resting his feet on a cross beam of weathered wood. "Most always get somebody to carry up river, never back down," he chuckled. "Call me, Billy Rowe. This here's Jim." He jerked a thick thumb at the first man.

Billy Rowe was fatter and older than Jim. His trousers tied around his bulging middle with fraying hemp.

He leaned over to scratch up some tobacco for his pipe, leaving chicken marks on the dusty planks.

Starlight and a rising moon now gleamed faintly through the open hatch, catching his flashing smile.

Captain Moore's voice rasped from above. "Billy Rowe, come up here and help me with this blasted anchor and sail. No more shifting time to waste getting this hulk up river." Both men scaled the ladder.

Jute, below, heard the winding winch and the anchor creak aboard. He felt the shifted weight as the sail began to pull the breeze, once the sheets were hoisted and the cleat lines fastened.

Jute enjoyed the freedom feel, moving at last. He glanced at Susu's huddled body and the bales that hid Momma safely in the hold. Going away up river, more like part of his plan.

Billy Rowe and Jim shimmied down the ladder, bare feet skimming the worn wooden rungs. They flopped down to rest on some empty burlap sacks.

"Your master?" asked Jute jerking his head toward the open hatch.

"Nope, I'm free," replied Jim, "and so is Billy Rowe. We works for pay." The proud ring of his words caught Jute with envy.

"How you happen to come free down here so near Virginia?" asked Jute in unbelieving tones.

"We was set free together," said Jim. "We come from the same home place." He leaned back and pulled at his cob pipe before continuing his story. "One morning we all go to the tobacco fields like usual. Old Master been sick. A house man come out from Old Mistress on a horse and say she want the overseer to come to town. He leave and go in town. After a while the old horn blow up at the overseer's house, and we all stop and listen, 'cause it's the wrong time of day for the horn to blow."

"We start chopping again and there go the horn again and again. The lead row man hollers, 'Hold up,' and we all stop an' listen. 'We better go on in 'cause that's our horn,' he hollers."

"We afraid we catch the devil from the overseer if we quit without him there, but maybe he's back from town and blowing the horn himself. So we line up and leave the fields like we're sposed to when the horn blows."

"When we gets to the quarters, we see all the old ones and all the children up in the overseer's yard. So we follow there, too. The overseer is sitting on the end of the gallery with a paper in his hand. He say, 'Stand close,' and he read off everybody's name and we see we all there."

"Setting on the gallery in a hide-bottomed chair was a man we never see before. He had on a big black hat and store clothes that wasn't no homespun, and they all over black. His hair was plumb gray and so was his beard. It come way down here but he don't look like he's very old cause his face is kind of fleshy and healthy looking. We find out later he is some kind of lawyer, but right then I think we all been sold off in a bunch."

"The man say, 'You know what day this is?' He talk kind and smile. We don't know so we just stand there. Don't no one answer."

"'This am Freedom Day for you,' he say, reading all our names off his big paper. It's a long time sinkin' in. We don't have to come and go by the horn no more. We don't need no more passes to leave the place."

"'I wants to bless you and hope you always stay with God. I tell you got all the rights and lief that any white folks got,' the man say, and then he gets on his horse and rides off."

"We all just watch him go down the road. Then we go to Mr. Saunders, the overseer, and ask him what he wants us to do? He just grunts and say, 'Do like you damn please. Master freed you with his dying breath, but get off the place to do it, lessin any of you wants to stay and help bring in the crop. You kin have your cabin and part of what you raise.'"

"Some folks stayed. Old Mistress move in town and the overseer he stayed, too. But Billy Rowe and me, we went on up river. Heard Captain Moore needed hands for his boat and we works here ever since. We gets all our eats and split one bale of tobacco each trip for what we can get at the other end. And keeps our mouths shut about folks like you," he added.

"I've got my freedom papers right here," said Jim. "Ain't nobody allowed to get hold of me."

Jute shook his head. He had a different dream, and he wouldn't settle for less. Canada—there everyone was free.

\* \* \*

Jute lay awake long after the shifting boat rocked the others to sleep. He'd never heard of anyone set free before. Free and working on the river. It was a new idea rattling his head. He thought until he too gave way to the cradled motion of the water.

Billy Rowe struck a metal cleat with his hammer at sunrise. Startled, Momma jerked up suddenly awake. Smelling the cooking food, close tobacco, and brackish river, she lay her head on the rags in the bow, retching sick.

Susu darted up the ladder to daylight and food before Jute could catch her. She clasped her hands, her eyes wide at the river opening up in the morning light. Shining water stretched between the high green banks. A roof or two pierced the trees, and some fields showed red-brown turned earth.

"You like the river, missy?" asked Captain Moore. He stood against the rail, a thick brown mug cupped in two hands for safety or against the morning chill.

Susu cringed toward the hatch. She's been told to stay below and out of sight!

"Hsst." Jute's face, his scowl an angry scar across it, showed in the opening at her feet.

"Let her stay," said Captain Moore. "Squat there," he added pointing to a small boat lashed to the cabin. Susu sat in the small boat, her knees drawn up, for most of the day. She ate the meals Jim brought her from a tin plate and cup, only leaving once to crawl below to make water into a slop bucket near the bales where Momma lay. Sweaty and sick all day Momma refused her food, her upturned eyes moon pale. She didn't seem to know who Susu was when she came near. Her lips moved without sound. She's praying, Susu thought. Praying that the boat won't sink, that those men won't follow us all this way, and Poppa will find us—somewhere, sometime.

Susu smiled at Momma, but Momma paid her no mind, her eyes still glazed. Could she see her? Susu wondered and was afraid. She crept into the snug and rocking tobacco crib long before it was really dark. She saw Jute climb the ladder in the night to go on deck for the first time that day. To feel the wind in his face as she had felt it, to see where they were going, to plan ahead.

She spent the second day as she had the first. Hidden in her perch above decks she grew used to the swaying boat and the wild birds' cry. They seemed to be following her as they swooped and darted into the boat's white wake.

Jim and Billy Rowe worked up on deck before dark calling to each other as they unwound the lines that lowered the fraying square sail. Before dropping anchor they let a small boat pass.

Then, as the barge nudged a solid dock, they motioned Susu to go below. Staying in the shadow of the cabin she hurried down to Jute.

"This here's where we leave," he said.

Jute almost carried Momma from her burlap bed. She seemed too limp to stand. He left her propped up on a bale near a door barred and cross-beamed above the water line.

"She'll feel to rights once we get on shore," he said to Jim more strongly than he felt. He'd never seen Momma like this. She didn't talk, ask where they were, or why. Her face burning and her mouth dry.

Unbolted, the cargo door swung out. Jim crawled through to catch the bales Billy Rowe tossed him. He piled them neatly under a broad shed roof, adding to other stacks already there.

Later, there was no sign of Captain Moore as Jim and Jute lifted Momma onto the dock. They laid her down behind the freight. Susu saw the bundle forgotten in the hold and tugging it to the opening she shoved it through till it landed on the dock. Jute turned at the sound of its muffled thud.

Turning back to his burden, he eased Momma through the shed door. Her skirt and legs dragged along the splintered wharf. She made no move, no effort to stand.

Jute and Jim grimly shared her weight down a pebbled path to a cellar door Jim seemed to have no trouble finding in the dark.

## CHAPTER FIVE

## Cousin James's Place

Jute never knew the name of the people in the Alexandria house. As Cousin James's Place, it became a bitter memory of more things he couldn't change.

The basement was damp with jars of fruit preserves and pickles lining raw wooden shelves. Beads of water gathered on the stone walls, running along shiny green moss to the dirt floor, wet from spring to spring.

Jim and Jute gently set Momma down between them. Susu's heart beat with the strangeness about her. She had struggled up from the dock unnoticed by the others, the bundle banging against her pumping legs. Momma's cheeks sucked in between each huge gasping breath, her lips no longer moving with silent words.

Susu's fingers tore the knotted cloth of Momma's winter shawl as she undid the bundle she had carried from the barge. Spreading it out, she placed her things at the top to make a pillow for Momma's head. She looked up at Jute, her eyes dry with fright. He moved Momma carefully, pulling at her dress until she lay upon the bed Susu had made.

"I'll tell the folks she's sick," said Jim, leaving as they had come through the cellar door.

"She's sick from the boat?" asked Susu, finding her voice at last, after Jim had left.

Jute didn't answer. He stood, his body taut, listening for sounds from the house above. They could only hear the harsh grate of Momma's breathing. Impatience growled in Jute's throat. He fingered his knife.

"Shut," he said gruffly, listening again to nothing. Exploding, he hit the side of his fist soundlessly against the wet stone wall, over and over, scaring Susu more.

"Now this," he muttered. "And Willett didn't tell me where from here," his anger taking shape against Ross Willett, the only one he could blame when the plan went awry.

Jute stooped and put a gentle hand on his mother's burning brow, smoothing it over and over softly, as Momma had brushed Susu's hair in the dark cave. Susu knelt near them. Tears trickled down her face. Momma would have prayed or moaned or sang. She could do nothing.

Jim came back, an oil lamp held high. Behind him, a woman dressed in brown shining stuff, held her skirts carefully away from the moldy earth. She dropped her skirts when she saw Momma lying on the shawl, and kneeling placed her hand where Jute's had been on Momma's head. Rattled breathing pierced the damp night; shaking the sick woman's entire body.

"She can't stay here, " she said.

"Back on the barge, Miss Julia?" mumbled Jim.

Jute stood beyond the shadows of the lamp where he had moved at the first sounds of their approach, fists clenched at his side.

"She must be brought into the house. A doctor must see to her. My brother would agree if he were here," said the woman.

Jim gathered up Momma, shawl and all. Carrying her like a babe, he trudged heavily up the cellar steps.

Jute looked to follow.

"Stay here," said Miss Julia softly at the door. "There's much that I need do." The cellar door closed silently.

Jute sat, braced against the dripping wall. Susu dried her eyes with her skirt. She wanted to bury her head in Jute's lap and have him stroke her head as he had Momma's. Never could tell what Jute would do. She stayed where she was, listening as he listened to the silent house above them. Hours crawled by, too long for Susu to fight the sleep that overcame her at last.

It was almost morning when the lamp returned, held this time by a house servant. She wore a clean white kerchief and apron starched to match like old Sarah had back home.

"Come," she said.

Jute and Susu scrambled to their feet and followed, up the steps, around the corner of the house, through a heavy outer door and into a dimly lit hall near some steep back stairs. Climbing them Jute looked hopelessly about, anger drained by the long silent watch below. The woman opened a door and stood back to let them pass through first.

Momma lay beneath a pile of quilts on a cot in a small dressing room without windows. The smell of boiling roots was strong in the steamy room. Her eyes were closed and her hands folded on the coverlet. No rasping breath tore at her chest.

"We tried sweat baths to break the fever," said Miss Julia, passing a white hand over her coiled hair, "but it was too late. She had no will to go on." Susu and Jute stared unbelieving at their Momma's still form.

"Why now?" Jute's brain rang out over and over. "Why now?" drowning out the rest of Miss Julia's words. Poppa sold, Momma dead, no route he knew ahead, and Susu! He looked at Susu standing beside the bed, twisting the rough homespun of her dress round and round her finger. Staring at Momma's peaceful face, just staring. Susu wishing they were home, Jute thought bitterly.

"Say thy goodbyes, child," said Miss Julia to Susu. "Thy mother must be buried before morning when the rivermen leave. I'll leave you alone with her a bit." The door clicked shut behind her.

Susu, saying nothing, touched her mother's folded hands. Poppa will never find us now, she thought. She looked shyly up at Jute for some sign of what to do. Swallowing was hard, even crying past.

Jute waited till they were alone. Bending down, he gripped Susu's shoulder hard and whispered in her ear. "We'll leave alone tonight," he said. "I'm not waiting for them and their plans. This is where their plans have led us." The old ring returned. Jute was in charge again.

"Can we see her buried?" Susu began.

"No time," Jute interrupted. "We're got to cut out now."

Still scared, but somehow reassured, by his strength Susu nodded, pressing back the questions of how and when. Jute would know. It was easier to leave Momma here than at the grave's cold edge.

Momma—she looked again at her Momma's peaceful face—and Susu was glad she was in a real bed, with quilts, not down in all the wetness of the damp cellar lying on her shawl. Maybe now Momma and Poppa would meet again. She began to make up a pretty place in her head, when Miss Julia came back.

"Thee must wait in the cellar till a packet can be arranged for, a safe one going up the coast," she said to Jute. "It may take days. The last one was seized and searched. We got the runners safely off just in time. That's where my brother James is now. Like as not you'll go up together with the last shipment."

"Yes'm," said Jute meekly, his manner fooling Susu not at all. His eyes flashed when he'd been told he'd have to wait longer here in the place where Momma died.

Down in the cellar Jute rewrapped their belongings, looking hard at the small tin box Mr. Willett had given him, Congrieve matches! About ready to dash them to the ground, Jute changed his mind and carefully stuffed them into the kettle rolled up with the heavy woolen shawl.

He grabbed Susu's hand. Together, they slid the door open a crack and crept out of the cellar running toward the river. The barge was still docked, the wharf deserted. The small boat Susu had crouched behind in the barge was riding high and empty, secured only to a post by a line looped through an iron ring.

Carefully Jute pulled it in and guiding Susu's elbow helped her climb aboard. He untied the knot and with a mighty heave sent the small boat drifting out across the river, between the anchored barge and the wooden dock. After they had passed the barge, Jute slid out the oars and pulled against the current toward the opposite shore. Susu, huddled on the bottom, looked up at him.

"We're getting free," he said to her, soberly through gritted teeth. "We're getting free alone."

## CHAPTER SIX

# Alone

Susu couldn't feel, couldn't think. She stared at a dark shape bigger than the others on the shore approaching fast. The landing bump sent her flying forward into the skiff, bundle scraping to the floor. She cried out as her elbow hit a sharp crack on the boat's sloping side.

"Latch on," said Jute, grabbing her roughly. He shoved her clear of the boat and with his free hand sent it spinning out into the current, bobbing empty.

Tripping on roots of water-logged trees growing at the river's edge, Susu scrambled up the bank. Her breath hard, bursting her ribs, she ran to match Jute's stride. Up the bank, suctioning mud grabbed her feet till she reached drier land above. No stopping Jute. Bent low through prickled brush he ran, not heeding branches scraping her face. She was pulled along behind him like a stone on her crab bait line. Her lower lip between her teeth, tears and sweat made slug-tracks down Susu's face. Her breath caught in with sobs she wouldn't let go. Jute wasn't going to hear her cry, she thought. She couldn't keep up, and still he dragged her along.

The land on the far side of the Potomac was rough. They had gone about a mile when Jute let go her hand and flopped down, panting from the effort of running and pulling her behind him with the bundle on his hip. He put his head down on jack-knifed knees to steady his heaving back. Susu, flung loose, stumbled a few steps before she fell on tangled matted grass, face down, hearing her sobs now, feeling her aching side pressed against the ground.

Jute lifted his head, his breath under control. He sniffed the air, the rich loamed smell of freshly turned earth.

"Shush," he said, finger on his lips. Again he heard it, the clank of a cow bell close in a field beyond the edge of the wood.

Susu rolled over and sat up, staring at him hard. There wasn't no one now in this world but Jute. No one to cook nor nothing. What was he figuring to do, sitting there sniffing and listening to the air? She shivered.

Jute looked at Susu huddled in the open, his plan cleared in his head. She was going to set to and make it with him. She got to; he'd see she did.

"We got a far way to go," he said. "Over them high hills we can't even see yet, an' cross rivers till we get to the big one called Ohio. Folks like us float right up there easy on rafts. I met a man who'd done that and he told me clear. No more walking or running. Right on up to Canada."

He watched her eyes struggling to believe him..

"But 'fore then," he added in a harsher voice, "we got a piece of running to do, sweating, hiding and scratching around for eats. No crying or hanging back. I'm not hauling you, Susu. No sir, you got to get there same's me — one foot, then t'other."

Susu straightened her back and nodded. She was hungry, but Jute'd said they had to scratch for food and she wasn't noticing him scratching yet, she thought.

"How come you know the way? You ain't never been there more'n me," she asked.

The sky was getting brighter towards the river. "See that?" Jute pointed to the lightening sky in the direction they'd come.

Susu nodded, slowly, not quite sure where to look.

"That morning sun now will always be at our right shoulder, and setting sun on our left. We keep a bead on Northwest, and we'll hit that river in a month or so."

A month... Susu reckoned on how long used to be a week. Honey on her corn cakes, and church every Sunday. Next day would start a new batch of washing with old Sarah. Took till Saturday to get them linens put back on the shelves of the linen room.

Days between mixed up in her head. Back home Momma brushed her hair on one of them and tied all those ribbons tight again — Momma — the sob of that thought caught her unbewares. It slipped out before she could shut her mouth, but Jute paid her no mind. He just went on.

"We travel at night mostly, in the farm country like this, sticking to tree lots and hedge rows. We kin move any old time of day in the wilds. Wish I had me a rifle for game, but this knife'll have to do. Happen we won't starve," he said, thinking of the dogs' throats slit while sleeping.

"What you fixin to do now?" Susu wanted to know.

"Pack some more miles 'tween us an anyone as knows we'se here," he said.

Jute got up, no longer pulling Susu's hand. He started out more slowly, sticking to the woods.

\* \* \*

Days they traveled through farm country in the still dark morning hours and early evening. Jute tied the bundle on a stick braced against his shoulder. They rested in heat of noon and again at night. Jute shook Susu awake, and in the dark they'd start a new day.

They ate at night from Jute's hoard in the bundle — dry bread and fruit, a bite of sausage roll, no more. They drank at any creek or spring they crossed. Jute seemed to think one meal enough. Susu almost forgot feeling the hard tight knot where her belly used to be. But she never got used to the push of moving, all the time forward, toward the setting sun, her legs torn by branches, her feet getting hard to the bone.

Sometimes when they stopped she slept at once. Sometimes she spread her treasures in a row, touching each with a finger as she counted them: the white pebble round as a wren's egg, a bright blue feather, an oyster shell from the river smooth on both sides, and her corn husk doll Poppa'd fashioned with a skirt made of real cloth scavanged from washing rags. And last, a little bottle no one seemed to want on the place, its stopper gone, brown letters standing up around the edge in a half moon shape.

They all fitted in her tin mug, stuffed around with moss to keep them there. Susu smiled and hummed a little when she played. All them pretty things still here, she thought, still mine.

* * *

That one day Susu spied the apples first, rows and rows of them through trees across the road, small and green.

A farm cart rattling in the distance warned them to lie low in the bush. Susu's mouth puckered almost tasting them hard green apples. She held her breath as the plodding hoofs of a brown horse pulled even with her unblinking eyes. The farmer, rosy cheeks under a rough home-woven hat, drove on, staring at the road ahead, clucking at his horse, thinking his own thoughts. Once out of sight Susu strained against Jute's tugging arm.

"A while yet," he warned, forcing her back again to wait some more, till even the faintest jingle of the harness died.

Jute went first; then beckoning her across the road, he filled his shirt and bundle with the still ripening fruit. They ate three times that day.

"Susu, quit jawing," said Jute as she reached into the pile for still another apple after they'd settled down that moonless night in a hillock near a running spring. The first few apples she'd eaten fast on the run, chomping up the whole thing before starting on the next.

That night they shared the last biscuit hoarded from Cousin James's cellar. Nothing left now but more apples — as many as the kettle held. One, saved till after dark, Susu ate slowly, sucking up the juices through her teeth. She kept the tiny pits curled in her hand. Finished, she poked six holes with her finger in the dirt near her head and buried them one by one in that secret spot. The hard hunger knot left her stomach that night, blown up and aching with green apples. She didn't care. There were more for morning and the next day.

The kettle, heavy with apples, was hard for Jute to lug. They pecked their way through hilly country with no trace now of farms or roads. Jute took the lead, following a steep hunter's track. They nibbled roots, berries and the last few withered apples rattling hollow in the emptying pot. Susu, always weary, could sleep whenever they stopped for breath, night or not. Jute sat up burdened with the worry of it all. Was this way leading them to the big Ohio?

Hatred drove him on. The men behind had as good as killed Momma. Her heart broke, and the baby fever coming on so quick. He'd had to leave with Poppa sold. He would have been next, and who'd have cared for Susu then? This way was right if they could keep going north far enough. Canada, as big as heaven, stretched out arms to Jute. He'd shake Susu, and they'd stumble on no matter what the time of day.

Susu got so her feet could go, even over the hard spots, leaving her mind free. One day she was drifting behind a bit, musing about having a real bed like the one Momma died on. A real bed and a room with a window. Same room day after day, to go to sleep in, wake up in, sunshine, rain.

Jute's voice broke through her dreams, lashing, twisting through the space between them.

"Susu quit laggin', somethin's up ahead. Fast water, hear?"

Standing, listening like a jack rabbit sensing danger, he began to sidle down hill till he reached the bank of a swift moving river, cut deep, forest on both sides.

"Is it the Ohio?" asked Susu not knowing what that was, just knowing it was important for Jute. "Naw, but you can't wade this 'un. Stay hidden. I'll scout around."

Susu crawled under a bush, eyes trailing Jute who'd disappeared upriver. He soon returned dragging two driftwood logs round about as his leg, bark worn off by scrabbling current.

"Lashed together with wild grape vine they'll make a fine raft." Susu wondered if Jute was going to ride too, but she'd learned better than to interrupt.

The log, secured with sturdy knots, pleased Jute.

"Sit astride," he said. "an' don't move none nor set it a'rockin. I'll lead by this loop."

With their bundle clutched between her legs, Susu sat carefully on the unsteady perch, one end already in the water.

Jute slid in, inching the raft behind him.

Soon he was pulling hard, making headway against the fast water although he lost some ground drifting a bit downstream with every stroke.

Won't matter, he thought, so I end up a bit lower, I'll make it up overland.

He looked up to gage where the pull might land him — about by that big gray flat rock at the water's edge. Getting closer.

Suddenly his world shattered, river, raft, Susu and all. A second measuring glance at the rock showed a man. A white man standing motionless next to it, holding onto a sturdy birch, watching Jute's progress.

Too late, pounded Jute's brain. Too late to change his course now.

Closer and closer to the rock, the river's force pulled him on.

Maybe we can outrun him, Jute chewed on the problem, thinking also of his knife. Let him make the first move.

Susu eyed the man standing on the far shore as unmoving as the pine stumps and mountain ash around him. He didn't look like the white men back home. He was dressed in tattered leather breeches with a face to match. An Indian maybe, she thought. A long hunting rifle and a powder horn hung at his side. He didn't lift it none or look like he was bound to.

She stared at him hard. They'd always run from men before. What made Jute think this man was safe? Susu couldn't tell but wasn't asking.

Jute swam, one arm guiding the bobbing logs across the last short stretch of river. The current rushed them near the flat rock where the man stood waiting. I'm a match for one lone hunter should he choose to fight, he thought. Susu glanced at Jute but couldn't see nothing new in his straining face.

"Whence come you?" asked the stranger as they pulled the raft ashore. No way to keep him from leaning down and helping beach the craft. His homespun shirt hung loosely on his tall spare frame. Red hair hacked off unevenly was tucked behind redder ears.

"Back aways," answered Jute, eyes on the rifle now leaning against a tree. That would come in handy for game. No one around. He could bury his knife as quickly in this man as in the dogs' soft throats. The thought slid through Jute's mind...

Susu hung back.

"Going far?" asked the woodsman.

"Canada," answered Jute, the word's proud ring was comfort in his ears.

"If you've not ate proper in a while you can stop with us the night."

Creeping Jesus. He said us. He's not alone, thought Jute. Together they followed a path along the shore. I'll just see how many there are.

The cabin stood square, made of peeled logs, a central chimney spitting smoke, some chickens scratching around a bone-dry yard.

"Folks around?" asked Jute guarded. Still time to grab the rifle and get.

"Just family," answered the man. "Sometimes weeks goes by before we see someone. Out there is Spruce Knob." He pointed to a distant peak rising higher than the others behind the small house.

"No folks between this holler and t'otherside. Only this here pass through the ridge."

He was a tall man. Ducking inside the door, he stood back for Jute and Susu to pass. Once in the cabin, Jute felt trapped.

Why does this man bother with us, he wondered? Maybe news of a price on their heads had got on ahead. Jute figured on it fast, like a man used to the wilderness and taking chances, he could sniff out danger when it lay ahead. No senses warned him here.

A woman, kneeling near the fire, looked up, saying nothing.

"Bondsmen," said the man, hanging his rifle and powder horn on pegs over the door. "Here to stay for the night." Bondsmen! Confound it! He'd labeled 'em like he knew the very name of the home place Jute had run so far to leave behind. Like they was on a string somehow and wouldn't never be really free.

A sudden scuffle above sent Jute's hand to his knife. Susu looked up to see three little yellow heads poking out from a loft.

"You can join the young'uns," said the man. "This here's Meg. There's cool water a plenty out back," he added handing Jute a dipper.

"Jute and Susu," said Jute, nodding in the direction of the loft.

He left to get some water, hearing the woman talk for the first time when the slatted door banged behind him. He stood a while to listen. Her voice strained with anger, her harsh whisper sounding like a stifled shout.

"Don't want no strangers staying here, coming with them dark faces and foreign ways. I told you so before. I said so last time them kind was passing."

"Just a half-growed man, Meg, and a wee'un like in age to Alice. Near starving by the looks of them."

"We got no food to spare," said Meg, her voice still flat and mad.

"Got enough. No one goes on to Spruce Knob past Streeter's place a'hungering. You know that, Meg, so quit your yammer."

Jute let out a sigh. He'd had a right feeling in his guts again. No danger here. She didn't want them, but Rob Streeter gave the orders.

When Jute returned from the well, Meg still knelt at the fire, her back stiff.

"Sit, boy," said Rob.

Jute sat at the bench and table near the cabin window. Slamming out the door, Rob muttered something about fixing the animals for the night.

Jute eyed the rifle still on its peg. Grab and run, grab and run, sang out his brain. Easy enough; no need to hurt no one. King's breeches, where's Susu at? Couldn't hear her saying nothing up there in the loft, but that's where she be at. Jute went on studying in his head, knowing he'd do nothing, just lean against the window wall looking. A lot he could do with a gun of his own.

He couldn't take from this man or hurt him none. He helped all folks cross the river. He'd said as much to his woman. Jute wondered at himself, trusting a white man, a stranger, his house as small and bare as his own. Just stop a bit till morning. Least-a-ways Rob Streeter wasn't telling him where to go or what to do.

The woman still didn't say nothing direct to Jute. She dished up rabbit stew and called the children down to eat. Susu followed them down the ladder to the table. They'd been playing in the loft, but no one spoke at supper. They spooned in the thin gravy and sopped it with hard flat bread. It tasted good to Susu, and she tried to make it last.

She looked up from her plate to see the others still eating. She twisted her fingers in her lap, quiet. Maybe they'd stay here, she thought. A rough nudge from Jute brought her to. The others rising, went to bed. The dusky light of the loft disclosed some ticking filled with straw. Susu and Jute shared one, the little ones another on the far side of the ladder opening. Meg scraped the dishes with a clatter, washing up outside the door. Susu couldn't hear Rob Streeter. He must be sleeping too.

\* \* \*

They left next day after hoe cakes. It was still dark along the trail. Over the ridge the wilds began. Trudging on, days became like one.

Sometimes they found berries on the scrabbly mountain ridges or mushroom fungus Jute knew they could eat, growing red and flabby on the trees.

The day Jute caught a coon, slow and rambling near a spring, he slit it up the back with his knife. That night they made a fire, no one to see the smoke. Their meat curled around the sticks and roasted, dripping fat sputtering the tiny flames. Jute's small tin of Congrieve matches from Mr. Willet dwindled as a snared squirrel and a quick-caught mountain bass followed the coon.

Days passed with nothing hot to eat. Nibbling tender roots, the tight knot came back to Susu, strong. A storm lasting near a week plastered her hair dripping to her head. Ribbons lost, she didn't like to touch it. Her hair always reminded her of Momma most — Momma and her soft loving hands. Her dress was torn, her bare feet hard as a skinned beech.

Jute never talked now. Just pushed ahead or slept, sharing food equal, saying nothing. Susu'd heard Streeter tell Jute to follow the North Star. Off-times wasn't none.

Susu saw Jute study where the moss grew on tree trunks and follow animal tracks to trace a spring. She watched him stretch snares for possum and knife fish. She slept with Momma's shawl around her, holding tight her corn cob doll.

Seemed like half a year'd gone by. Jute knew it'd been little more than a month. Christ-a-sunshine, where was that river? The country was smoothing out some, with farms between fields stretching to the woods.

Six eggs! Jute tucked them in his shirt one dawn, before an old dog came yapping sniffing him out, his hind legs stiff with sleep. Jute outran him easy, one egg cracked, sliding down inside his breeches. The others he and Susu gulped raw.

Setting out that morning, still trailing mainly west, Jute saw the many roof tops of a town, before glimpsing the flat band of water shining beyond.

"Ohio," he whispered. Then, to Susu still behind, "the Ohio," not believing it himself. They ran to a bluff overlooking the river.

"It's really there," Jute murmured. "Just like they said." Susu looked up at him. The open wonder on his face wiped off the scowl she'd grown accustomed to. It made Jute seem a stranger in her eyes, smiling almost.

Flopping in the tall weeds they could see poleboats pulled up below, steamboats with people buzzing round like market day, horses hitched to waiting carts, women with sunbonnets and baskets buying things from stalls set up in rows.

"Hold on," said Jute, pulling Susu back, "while I hatch on what to do."

## CHAPTER SEVEN

## The Ohio

A crackle through the trees warned them of the burro's approach before they saw the boys or heard their voices. Crouching low behind the boulder, Jute and Susu peered at two boys gathering sticks, loading an animal already buried under a pile of ragged kindling.

"I'm doing all the work," said one boy. "Let me lead him a while."

"Stubborn jackass," said the other. "It's harder leading. I'm wore out already with the pulling." His sandy hair stuck out all over like a dry haymow.

"Let's lunch," he said.

Susu and Jute held their breath, twin tiny gasps escaping as from a pricked balloon.

"Naw, let's finish first, then swim a bit before heading back."

They went on, picking up sticks as they went. The unwilling burro tugged and kicked in turn.

"How can we get on one of them boats, Jute?" Susu asked when the boys were out of sight.

"Shut," said Jute, sharp-like, bothered by her asking the one question he kept asking himself. How do I find a safe boat to take us up to Canada?

He studied the town some more. Many steamboats for passengers and barges were tied up to the wharf. A row of black dock workers, each with a sack on his back, strode up a board plank into one of the waiting boats. Coming back again and again for another load they worked in the heat of day. If I could just ask one of them, he thought.

49

He wondered if they were free like Billy Rowe and Jim or if they had a master nearby. He saw no chains or overseer keeping them there. The mounting pile of burlap sacks grew on the flatboat deck. Still, the men marched on.

The sun was lower round the river bend when a shrill whistle, echoed by a bell downstream, brought to a halt the ant-hill of activity below. Women hurried off, their baskets heavy, disappearing down roads hidden by walls, into waiting carts. Some joined lounging men and children who'd been playing in the busy streets. Some children, left alone when the whistle blew, picked up their hoops and ropes, fixing to join their elders down the street.

Stalls were emptied, covered with canvas, weighted down with stone and bricks against the tugging river breeze. The rising wind brought the smell of dead fish, boiling tar, and cooking food up to Jute. Same smell as round St. Mary's City Pier back home.

Dock workers, finished loading, drifted around the corner of a pitch-paper shack with a tin stove pipe sticking up like a waving hand. Jute waited. The men didn't come around the other side. Mayhap they lived inside. He waited until the movement around the river bank had stopped.

"Stay here," he said to Susu. "I think I can make it down there without nobody seeing me. Watch sharp; I'll beckon for you to follow if it's all right to come."

Down the bluff he crawled to the corner of the shack where he'd last seen the men. The door on the far side toward the river was open. Flies swarmed around a skinny tan cur lying right beneath the stoop. He didn't lift an ear as Jute came sneaking up, trying to hear what was going on inside.

Jute smelled the cooking grease and sharp corn liquor before he made out the figures of men crowded around a table with a smoky tallow lamp. A man, lounging on a bunk on one side of the shack, looked at Jute framed in the doorway.

"No work, tad! We got this job bedded down."

"Who sent ya?" joined another voice from an upper bunk.

Jute swallowed and stepped inside. "Be needing passage down to Cincinnati," he said. "I'll work, join you, or whatever you say." He looked back over his shoulder and moved sideways out of the doorway. The habit of not being seen was strong.

He jerked his shoulder in the direction he'd come. "I left me a youngster, Susu, back up on the hill. I can do a man's work, and she don't eat near nothing. We're needing a ride to Canada," said Jute. Nobody was answering. "To Canada," he said again, running out of words. He breathed tight, looking into the black faces around the lamp.

"To Canada," sneered the man on the bunk. "that all, why ain't we all agoing on this picnic? Hosses tails, boy, it ain't just that easy. You're needing passes and freedom papers." The men laughed.

"We're hired out here slack season by our masters," said a short fat man at the table shoveling food into his mouth between words. "The steamship company pays us two dollars a week if you works hard and your pass is in order, and gives our master one dollar. It only takes eight hundred dollars to buy your freedom! Living in this heap costs four bits a week just eating money." He looked back at his cards, shoving his plate aside.

"Ever seen Canada anyway, boy? Freezing weather from August till July, with no one to give you boots or work," joined in another man at the table. "I seen men come back here they's toes and fingers just froze off in one winter. No need to get there so quick. Go back where you comes from."

"I'm fixin' to go on," said Jute, his jaw a stubborn line. Ain't got no place behind, nowhere, and a sister not yet ten to care for. She got no one but me."

"We can keep you for the night, maybe slip you aboard a packet afore long." Jute hadn't noticed that man before, leaning near the stove, his hands shoved in his belt. He was thin and short, lighter than the others. His hair grew funny down his neck like a furry animal Jute once saw drinking from a spring.

His voice soft, curling round the words, "Bring the young'un and stay here, boy. There's room a'plenty on the floor behind the stove."

Two men looked up, as if to disagree, but said nothing. Something warned Jute — these were his own kind, and yet they weren't, living here slave and working for pay. So near the river but not going on up to Canada. He left the cabin, muddled.

"I'll get Susu," he told them, starting for the bluff. Once around the corner, he sneaked on back to the edge of the shack, bent over, his ear against the pitch-paper.

"What'd you go do that for, Del? I'm not fixing to live here with no kids," said an angry voice.

"Get sent up and whipped for dealing with fugitives like him," said another.

"Ain't like that at all," said the soft curling voice of the short man. "Come morning we show up on the dock. We tell Mister Conrad all about them. Should be fifty dollars on the boy at least. We see we gits our split."

"Aw come on, Del, they's young," was drowned out in the shuffling cards and clinking sound of a bottle passing around.

Jute didn't stay to hear more. Skinning up the bank, he grabbed Susu's hand.

"Quick!" he said, running low as he had the first day near the Potomac, bundle clutched to his curving stomach.

Susu, wide-eyed, glanced over her shoulder. Wasn't nothing following Jute but the terror in his voice was catching. She ran behind him, no need to pull. Along the brow of the hill they went, leaving the last straggling roofs of the town behind. Startled, a pheasant family flew in their faces. They ran until their pounding legs and thudding temples made the whole world swervy, black.

"We'll sit a spell, then push right on tonight," said Jute, wiping his sweaty face on the edge of a ragged shirt.

Where to? thought Susu, but she didn't ask.

# CHAPTER EIGHT

## Pell Knickers

They kept on, following the river. Jute stopped a mite listening now and then, but they heard no crackles of a sly approach.

"What men could have tired full bellies, fat enough to let fifty dollars slip away, or maybe they were just fooling about the money, knowing I was listening." Jute'd never know and took no chances. He'd have to figure a way to get across the Ohio and just strike north on foot some more.

His eyes roved over Susu resting there. She'd got skinnier, and quiet, didn't chatter none like she had at home. No complaining neither. She looked like she could make it on foot alone with him.

The sun was almost up when they stopped for the day, some choke cherries and sassafras roots their only food. Jute set a squirrel snare he'd made of vines and pointed out a hollow in some brush where they could lie hidden from the path. He tucked the shawl about her legs, more tender than before.

"Sleep now," he said, putting his body in front of hers so he'd be seen first if anyone should travel this tangled path above the river. He slept, too, most of the day.

✷ ✷ ✷

Jute checked his squirrel snare come evening. No luck, again, but no men neither. The more miles he put between himself and that town the safer he felt. Treachery there; greedy men with only thoughts of money and liquor. Jute felt safer alone with Susu, but tired too. Pushing on to Canada without no boat to ride. How far it was he didn't know.

"Come, Susu, we'll sup later," he said, hoisting the empty kettle on its stick. They trod the dim path, the river still a landmark down below. No food all night! Jute found a spring near daybreak, following damp animal tracks to where it bubbled free.

"Drink full," he said, and looping his net around a bush, he set the snare once more before sleeping.

A high pitched giggle woke him that afternoon. Another giggle shushed in the middle.

"Pell Knickers! Where you at! There's wolves and bears up there by that spring. Come back, you thorny twig!"

Jute sprang up. Susu's eyes opened too, almost even with two round brown ones blinking in a round brown face. One finger stopping up his mouth and knickers drooping to his ankles, a staring boy of three or four stood saying nothing. His mother pushed her way impatiently through the brush. Reaching out a hand, she swatted the little one on his rump sharply before noticing Susu and Jute crouched against discovery. After a gasp her breath came back.

"Laws," she said. "You give me a start. Pell Knickers, quit your roaming ways." Her hand latched firmly to the little boy's, she stepped around the muddy water of the spring.

Her brown eyes warm and friendly, her face, as round and soft as the child's, was split by a wide grin. Strong white teeth showed as she talked.

She's a friend, thought Susu, wishing she could hug the woman around the waist where a flowered apron stretched across the big belly.

About to drop another, noted Jute.

"All alone?" She nodded at Jute and Susu.

Caught unawares, Jute found he wasn't scared. If she has the same idea as them men, we'll take heel like we done before, he thought.

"Traveling on," said Jute, stronger than he felt. He followed the tiny boy as he led along a narrow path to where it stopped against a two-rail fence. "Figgering on how to get on down river," he added to the woman's back.

"Pa'll know," she said, helping the boy through the rails of the fence. She nimbly climbed up and threw her short legs over, jumping down on the far side, lightly, for her added weight.

Jute and Susu scrambled over, too. Still time to run, thought Jute.

"Pa's setting traps," said the woman, picking her way through rows of summer squash, sweet potatoes and beans. Susu wanted to scoop up handfuls of the growing vegetables. Leaning towards a row of beans, she was jerked upright by Jute, yanking the back of her dress so hard it like to tore off in his hand.

"Come in a spell."

The cabin faced the river, some big trees shading its roof. Smells of drying wool and frying corn brought water to Susu's eyes. Just like home. Susu flopped down on a string bed before she'd been asked to sit.

"Hungry little one?" asked the woman, tucking a strand of Susu's ragged hair behind her ear with one plump hand. The youngster stood staring, finger still in his moist red mouth.

Jute, always caged inside, kept eyeing the door.

Stirring a kettle set back on the fire to simmer, the young woman dipped a mug of barley soup out for Susu and another for Jute. The hot steamy liquid made tears spill over into Susu's mug. Like to stay here, thought Susu. Don't care about traveling that river, never!

\* \* \*

Crunching steps in the yard made her press against the sagging strings and logs of the bed on which she was sitting.

"That'll be Pa," said the young woman, reaching for another mug of barley soup. "He'll find you a way."

Pell Knickers ran to his daddy when the door opened. Burying his sweaty face between his father's knees he clung to both legs.

Susu jumped off the string bed. She inched over to where Jute was standing, until, hidden behind her brother, she could peep out at the big man without being seen. Tall and dark, Pell Knickers's Pa had a straight back and the bulging muscles of a man used to hard work.

"Pell Knickers found these folks at the spring," said the woman, setting the tin mug on the scrubbed boards of a center table.

"Set," said the man to Jute. He patted the small curly head at his knee and drew a stool up to the table. "What be your business up at our spring?"

Susu shivered. Would he turn them in for money, too, like Jute'd said about the others?

Jute watched the man begin to spoon up the hearty meal, before he, too, took a stool and sat opposite Pell Knickers's Pa. He told his story from way back when Poppa was sold. The words, starting slowly at first, stumbled over each other like water over rocks in a small steep stream.

He told about Mr. Willett and the night spent hidden in the pent; his raging quiet on the island filled with the fear of snakes; the barge; ma's dying; all the miles and days over the mountains; the cabin folks; and the near escape from the black dock workers who would've turned them in for fifty dollars. And now the big river they'd heard about, shimmering in the sight of this cabin, and no help to them at all! No way to ride it up to Canada.

"Hold on, boy," interrupted the man, "not so fast. There's mor'un one way to make the river work for you. Name's Matt. Have you ate some of Sarah's fixings here?"

Jute nodded. His hands clutched the table's edge, the tightening knuckles giving away his impatience. Juniper, man, he thought, this ain't no hog killing party. We've got to get on now!

Matt and Jute sat in silence while Sarah took away the mugs, returning with a plate of red beans and tin cups of cider from trees out back.

"Hold on, boy" Matt repeated. "I don't know nothing about Canada, but there's a fellow down at the harness factory sweeps up nights, like I do days. Simple Luke. They say he helped other folks scampin' up north. He might have an idea. Yep, Luke Brown might have an idea for you."

Jute couldn't stand to wait. He wanted to hunt up this Luke Brown right now, but there wasn't a way to make Matt move tonight. He'd pulled a cob pipe out of his jeans, stuffed and lit it before sitting down on his cabin step staring out at the river, so near the door.

Matt liked to talk. Now with a ready ear nearby he rambled on about his own pa buying his freedom and this piece of land from extra money he earned cutting down trees; settling in sight of the river; seeing the boats always on the move, but never moving himself. Matt said he didn't want to go nowhere neither.

Jute tried to understand this feeling of content he'd met in other folks, but gave up, and listened to the birds over the water and the woman inside singing, as she bedded Susu down alongside Pell Knickers. The slap of her wet cloth against the tin basin and the clatter she made sounded like home.

Susu woke first the next morning, knowing she was inside on a bed, a real bed, all curled up with Pell Knickers huddling into her back. It felt good. She could tell by the breathing sounds that they were all asleep in the small room. The Ma, Pa, Pell, and even Jute, under one roof. Susu liked the feel of it.

But just looking at Jute, even sleeping, she knew he was pushing to be on the move. Lying on some rugs by the fire, one hand loose behind his head, seemed he'd just lied down a spell and could jump up and be out the door if anyone stirred. He was that uneasy.

Sarah gave Susu a hug when they left, after porridge was eaten. She held Pell Knickers's hand and waved as Matt, Jute and Susu walked down the track to the river. Susu's steps lagged. Sure hankered to stay a spell in one place.

The smell of the harness plant drifted up long before they saw it, tanning leather rising rancid on the summer air.

"You folks stay here. Hide good," said Matt. "I'll ferret out Luke and send him back to you when the way is clear. Can't trust just anybody with ransoms paid and talk of them spreading."

Susu and Jute crawled through the brush to where they could glimpse the river and the path. Unseen from both, they looked out at the boats. The big ones hooted around the bend. Some had people crowded near the rails and smoke stacks shooting think black smoke. There were small barges like Captain Moore's with the sails puffed out. Sometimes they could hear the shouting, laughing men calling on the decks as they went by. Small skiffs, poled by one man, hugged the shore.

Jute's knife flashed as he whittled a sharp point on the stick he held. He jabbed it into the ground again and again, digging up a patch of earth where he lay. He didn't talk to Susu.

How come? he thought. How come these folks get to ride on the river, free as you please? And we keep hiding in bushes, asking for help and waiting—waiting all the time for others to know the way.

## CHAPTER NINE

## Simple Luke

The bushes parted as Luke waded down the path as if he didn't care who knew he was coming. His fat, dark tan, freckled face grinned down at Susu. Three chins wobbled when he moved. He drooled a yellow string of slime from one corner of his mouth. Stopping to mop a balding forehead with his dirty white handkerchief, he stopped the drool as well.

"Traveling, eh?" he said to Jute, chuckling to himself as if it was a joke only he knew. "Traveling up north is good in this weather."

Jute stopped whittling and sprang up, stowing his knife in his belt, hand on its handle just in case. His eyes roamed over Luke's flabby form in disbelief. This didn't look like a man could help him none. This giggling fool didn't know enough to be quiet on the open path to the harness plant!

"You've got to know how to go from here," Luke said, bending over, his cackle gone. Jute realized right off he'd been wrong guessing him to be a fool. Luke bent his head now talking fast and serious like he didn't have time to say anything twice.

"There's a family leaving tomorrow. I could stow the young one with them. No place for you there," he added.

"We go together," said Jute set, stubborn. Luke seemed to know what he was talking about, but Jute wasn't for separating now.

"Yes, together," said Luke, his eyes on Jute's thin bones, made sharper by the long spell without proper food. "Can you stoke a hefty shovel full of coal?"

"I'm stronger than I look," said Jute. "I can do a man's work and have on the home place tending tobacco."

"Little Missy'll have to be fixed up some. She'll be traveling with a white family as one of their own. Luke turned and jerked his head for them to follow. His private laugh returned, shaking his shoulders as he waddled in front of them. His head lolled with each step. The fool again.

Jute had a mint of questions to ask. Susu couldn't tell what this man was all about, but they followed quietly and quickly to where the path branched away from the river and became a pebbly road.

Still following, thought Jute bitterly. Still beholden to almost anybody. Luke, one minute serious, next a laughing clown of a man, said he had a place—darn fool sounding place—Susu and some white folks, going together, but not together. Still, they had to follow. No other choice now!

Luke stopped at the small side door of a barn, close to the road. Once painted red, its paint had long since faded, leaving pink patches mixed with yards of rough gray wood. The corner of a white house showed beyond a hedge of lilac bushes, spliced by a sagging white gate. Luke stepped inside. Susu and Jute followed.

It was like no other barn Susu had ever seen. Inside, three white painted iron beds were made up with blankets. The only other things within the musty room were packing cases and trunks with the lids thrown back, spilling out clothes, hats, dresses and shoes of all sizes, jumbled about, some trailing on the dirt floor. Bales of hay and a farm cart stood near double doors, barred from within. A skirt and a broken hoop hung crazily by its hem over the farm wagon's wooden rimmed wheel.

Luke slid a stick through the drawstring latch of the small door they had entered. He put his ear against the worn boards and listened, then straightened up again, his serious side now showing through the crinkled eyes and slacklipped grin.

"Don't mind Luke," he said. "Simple Luke." He grinned and slobbered and giggled and scratched his fat bald head.

Jute could see now that it was all an act, a blasted fine act, turned on at will to make him look a fool.

"No one pays Luke no mind, and I can slip in where folks with passes can't get at," he explained. "Now, about those clothes."

Luke could move fast when he had a mind to. Sorting through the boxes and trunks, he pulled out two dresses about Susu's size, one, dark gray and black braid and buttons; the other, dark all over. Both made of fine material and stitching like the Fahnstalk's clothes at home.

"The bonnet'll be the hardest," said Luke. "See if you can find a dark one her size. I'll get some food and bring Becky to help you dress." He pulled the latch to and was gone before Jute could ask the many questions rattling his brain.

Susu looked at Jute for permission to touch the fine clothes.

"Go on," he said. "You heard the man. Look for a dark bonnet."

Susu smoothed the fine stuff with one finger first. Feathers and velvet. Silky soft cloth she'd never touched before. In the wash house at Glen Mary she'd worked with the linens.

She picked up a cream colored bonnet with green feathers. Dark, he'd said. She dug deeper, loving the musty lavender smell of the clothes she discarded one by one, until near the bottom of the first trunk she found what she'd been searching. A bonnet of plain black taffeta, not too big for her. She set it on her head and looked slyly at Jute. He laughed silently and slapped his knee.

"Don't know where you'd be going in that rig," he said. "You'd frighten a hen out of her eggs for sure."

Susu reached up and felt the tangled mass of her hair, frizzing out in strands, they kept the bonnet from setting on her head proper-like. She sat down with the bonnet cradled on her lap and waited for Luke's return. He came back all business, tapping for Jute to unlatch the door. With him was a tall, thin woman in a black dress and apron.

Momma'd worn a black dress, tending the house babies. Susu remembered Momma, looking tall and thin, sorta like that woman, 'cept her black braid wound round into a fat knot, her head held up straight. Momma'd always walked as if she had a basket to carry on her head.

Susu was shaken out of her sad thoughts when the woman picked the bonnet from Susu's lap and plopped it on her knotted hair. She stepped back to see the effect. She didn't laugh at her like Jute had done.

"I'm Becky," she said. "Tsk, tsk, tsk, lots of work before this one can pass as any part of that Templeton family. Stand down child! Don't you have any underpinnings?"

Susu hung her head as Becky slipped off her ragged dress and slung a blanket around her bare shoulders. She sat down on the bed watching Becky bustle about the barn lifting a large tin basin off a nail on the wall. She set it on a low wooden packing case and left the barn by the small side door.

Susu could hear Luke and Jute talking about dressing her up and traveling on one of those big boats along with some white family in mourning. Least aways that was what she thought they was saying. Susu glanced wildly at Jute. Would he be there? He'd said down by the river bank that they'd stay together, but no one was talking about Jute dressing up in those fine clothes from the big trunks.

Becky returned with some water, cloths, and soap.

"Get in there and soak," she said to Susu, tipping her steaming heavy pail into a big tin tub. "Whilst I find something for you to wear under your dress, rummage out some gloves, and tack a veil to this bonnet here.

"It was hard at first for Susu to get her feet into the hot water, but she climbed up into the tub and sat there wondering what to do next. Once wet, she kept her teeth from chattering by rubbing the soap hard over her arms and folded legs. The soap stung her scratched shins, fast cooling water made her shiver.

"There," said Becky, laying the things she'd found in a row on one cot. "Step out. We'll dress first and fix your hair last."

She rubbed Susu dry and held up long trousers of thin white stuff with a ruffle on the bottom. A shift and petticoat, a might too long, were tied up about her tiny waist with ribbon. The gray dress was the better fit. When all those small black buttons were fastened, Susu felt stiff. Her arms stuck out like they were hitched to splints. She wasn't sure she could sit down. Becky helped her pull on some silk socks and buckled shoes so big they had to have rags stuffed in the toes to keep them on. Susu felt so strange she wanted her own dress back, even if it was all over mud, with torn places gaping down to her knees.

Becky stood behind her and brushed out Susu's hair. Her fingers didn't feel soft like Momma's, but she stayed with it till the brush ran smooth. Instead of making many little braids, she flattened it all back, held with pins that pricked Susu's scalp. She tied the bonnet on, but now it had a veil hanging in front, so dark Susu could hardly see Jute across the room.

"See here," Becky said. "This family is traveling on the Isle of Green, one of the biggest steamboats on the river. It goes all the way to Cincinnati. They're supposed to have a dead Pa in the box they're taking up home to bury, only he's one of our own and won't be dead for a long time unless something goes wrong. The lady's supposed to be yer Ma. Keeps your mouth shut and your head down. Pull your mitts over your hands when you're out where folks can see.

Jute'll be stoking coal in the hold so don't fret none if you don't see him. Now study on walking and sitting like the white folks you've seen. Mind you, don't trip none over them shoes."

Jute and Luke were shining up the farm wagon when someone knocked on the double doors. Luke slid the bolt and opened them wide enough for two men carrying a polished coffin with brass handles on their shoulders. They led a spotted gray horse. Clanking in they set their load down on the floor. The horse nibbled hay as the men talked.

"If I can just nail some slat up here under the lid so it won't close proper, I'll have me some breathing space inside and a good rest," said the younger man. His hair was cropped so short his scalp shone through. "How about some eats?" he asked, lifting the coffin lid. He took out bread, and a long slab of cold pork, as well as the hammer, slats of wood and nails he needed to do the job on the coffin.

They all shared the food, tearing off hunks of bread, waiting for the short haired man to cut slices of the cold meat.

"How can you plan like this?" asked Jute, jawing down the cold meat. "Where'd this stuff all come from?"

He pointed towards the cart, coffin, clothes, and even the iron beds so out of place in the run-down barn.

"Becky and Joe here used to work on this place with a pile of others. It was one of the best farms in Galia County owned by a family named Morris. Mrs. Morris helped a pack of our people who were traveling north in all kinds of ways before she died leaving Becky and Joe the house and enough money to go on with her work. We're headed to Cincinnati with Nate. Not too much trouble to slip in a few more members of the Templeton family whiles we're at it."

Joe, the older man who'd helped to carry the coffin, was fixing it now. He didn't say much but worked quickly, his big hands stowing away some leather straps to bind the lid so it wouldn't fly open on the trip.

"Who planned all this?" asked Jute, still puzzling over all the trappings — clothes, coffin, even the gray horse switching at flies as he chomped his hay.

"Simple Luke took over the planningwhen old Mrs. Morris died. Most people think this place is run down and empty. We cover our tracks pretty good."

## CHAPTER TEN

## Point Pleasant

Susu hung onto a plump hand covered with a silky black glove and thought only about her feet. One buckled shoe after the other, she mounted the gang plank of the Isle of Green, her heart tight and her throat dry. People surged around her. Baggage thumped on board below. The throbbing pulse of the engine and milling crowd of waving bystanders were just a blur. Becky had told her again, just before they left, not to trip over her big new shoes. She knew her bonnet and veil must not fly up and show her face. What would happen if it did was too frightening to imagine.

All the way to Point Pleasant Susu had sat on the seat of the farm wagon between Mrs. Templeton and her grown son, John. Mrs. Templeton was a slight, rounded woman who smelled of dry rose leaves and camphor. Long gray hairs escaped her black bonnet when she threw back her veil for a closer look at Susu and Jute.

"Stay next to me, say nothing, and keep your veil down at all times," she'd said softly at last, after studying Susu carefully, tipped her head this way and that toward the light. Her fingers grasped Susu's chin. "For gracious sakes, keep your arms down and not stuck out like a scarecrow."

Her son John, tall and silent, held the reins in his gloved hands and said nothing as the horse jogged on.

Susu was glad she didn't have to travel in a box like Nate, all fastened down with leather straps and only slits for air. How stiff she'd be not moving for fear someone would guess she wasn't dead. How scary to be all alone in the dark. Joe and Jute rode on the back step, ready to hoist the coffin when they arrived at the dock. Once on board she still clutched the lady's hand. Mrs. Templeton stopped to speak to a whiskered man with gold braid on his hat. They followed his directions down a steep stair and a long corridor so narrow Susu had to walk behind with no steadying hand to hold.

Mrs. Templeton opened a numbered door and turned to Susu standing there. "Come on child, don't be afraid. You'll be alone here in the cabin with me till Cincinnati," she said.

Once inside, Susu looked at the bunks, hitched to the walls like her bed at home. A small round window, way up high, showed nothing but a patch of blue sky. "Take off your dress and shoes and get in the upper bunk," Mrs. Templeton said to Susu in a hushed, kindly voice. "You're supposed to be feeling poorly this whole trip."

Susu's fingers fumbled with the black buttons. It was hard to bend her elbows in the stiff gray sleeves. The mitts kept her fingers from working right. She'd freed the top button and was attempting to undo the second when footsteps stopped outside their door. Mrs. Templeton turned a key in the lock just as a sharp knock came once, then once again.

Calling out, "Come back later," she hustled Susu out of her bonnet, dress and shoes, then hung the dress neatly on a hook on the wall lining the shoes beneath it. Mrs.Templeton pulled back the covers and helped Susu into the upper berth between crisp white sheets, tucking the covers up over her head.

"Keep your head under the covers at all times," she said, turning the key again before sitting down on the lower berth to wait for the steward's return.

The gang plank cranked aboard, the cabin shifted and shuddered as the Isle of Green pulled out into the channel, its paddle wheel churning a pulse-beat under the quickening ship.

Mrs. Templeton flung wide the door when the steward returned but stood in his path as she gave her order, "Some camomile for my little girl, tea and biscuits for me. She's not been well and this motion will not help." She passed a hand over her eyes. "This is a sad trip for us all without harm coming to little Melissa. I don't want her disturbed."

"Yes ma'am," said the steward, his eyes passing over her mourning garb without interest.

It was not hard to keep her head down as the sky turned slowly black in the little window. The twisting boat under Susu made her queasy and she gratefully pulled the clean sheets around her shoulders and slept.

* * *

Jute marched onto the lower gang plank as told, stripped to the waist, a shovel braced on his shoulder, his bundle under his other arm. An officer with a pad and pencil ticked off men's names as they strode by without looking at their faces.

"Tom Bullen," sang out Jute as planned.

Joe, head stoker, came last. He handed in their passes and waited as the men shuffled through, counting out loud. Jute followed the first man down into the hold.

Later, shoulders tired from shoveling coal into the yawning furnace, Jute stopped to pour a dipperful of water over his head and drank the better part of the next, before taking his short turn resting on one of the narrow wooden shelves which followed the curving lines of the boat's side. His muscles, though aching, were helping to bring them closer, closer, through his efforts. No longer taking the soft way waiting for some white man's order. He raised his strong arms overhead, hands clasped, letting himself think on victory a beat.

Spreading clothes from his bundle to pillow his head, eyes burning from the steamy smoke, Jute peered through the gloomy boiler room at two men now firing the engine's greedy jaws. There was only one lantern and the open fire for light. Gritty coal dust settled everywhere. He could feel it sticking to his sweaty palms, trickling down his face to drip on his dampening chest. It grated between his teeth and formed a dusty path beneath his feet.

He wanted to ask the other men if they were free or slave, and why they didn't walk off the boat at Cincinnati like he was planning to do. He'd noticed some chains and iron rings above his bunk, but Joe'd told him to say nothing that'd draw attention to himself, even if the white boss man was above deck out of hearing. He'd have to watch and learn, same as he always had, thought Jute.

* * *

A soft knock woke Susu. The window showed dark but it must be early evening because Mrs. Templeton, still dressed, was sitting near a lamp held to the wall by a metal bracket. She opened the door, and a bustling woman shoved past her near the table and small chair which filled the tiny stateroom.

"I heard your husband was dead below and you're cooped up here with a sick youngster. I came to spell you for a bit. Take a few turns around the deck. This evening breeze will do you good."

"I'm feeling poorly myself," said Mrs. Templeton, trying to discourage the stranger. The woman proved not easy to turn away.

"I buried my first husband not three years back. Married again last Christmas," she said. "I've nursed plenty people through this and that. The name is Grindel now, Polly Grindel. I always say the best thing for the water complaint is a stiff bout of evening breeze."

Mrs. Templeton planted herself firmly between the woman's solid form and the quiet hump Susu made in the top berth. She lowered her voice, nodding her head toward the bed.

"I think she has the jaundice that caused my man to pass away. Her tongue's turning dark, and her eyes yellow. If she goes, too, I pray the Lord will give it to us all. No use remaining alone now my son's grown. Buried the littlest one down home. I'm taking Mr. Templeton to lie in a plot with people of his own name. Might be the last thing I do."

She poked her face close to the visitor's. "Nice of you to come. Most folks would be afraid, sickness 'n' all."

The woman mumbled her regrets, leaving with measured haste. Mrs. Templeton lowered the wick until the lamp sputtered and went out. Before undressing for the night, she turned the key once more, locking the solid stateroom door.

Most of the two days passed as all work time did for Jute. Sleep, work, eat, then sleep again. He spelled the other men in the cabin, working shifts, shoveling the coal. One thing made it a nightmare time Jute never would forget. Every night the boat shuddered to a halt.

"Lock them up, Joe," a voice called down when they stopped at the first large town down river to take on more passengers and freight.

Each man put one hand through a metal ring fastened to the ship's hull above the row of bunks. A chain, drawn through them all was tightened, pinning them there like trapped rats until the ship was ready and moving again. Jute tried pulling his hand through, the first time, but the metal noose above his wrist jerked more tightly. No use. The harder he pulled, the tighter the chain bit into his flesh. First time chained, he thought, chained on my way to freedom.

The shame of being fastened like a cur burned in Jute's brain. With anger twisting his belly like a knife, he hated the white men who ran this ship. He looked around at the men near him, half hidden in the gloom, their arms pinioned to the wall. Some slept as if it was a welcomed respite to the heavy toil of the long day.

Didn't they feel degraded by it all? Their meek acceptance made Jute want to spit and bellow out a curse at those above who gave the orders. A warning look from Joe kept him still.

The next time he didn't even try to wrench his hand free, just put it through the ring like the others. He woke up grasping the strong metal hoop. Jute never got used to being chained. His gorge rose in anger every time the order came when the ship stopped for the night.

Joe bent lower than usual the third day when they were stoking coal together. He turned his head as he shoveled so he could whisper up toward Jute's ear. The hissing steam escaping from a valve near the top of the boiler made it hard for Jute to hear Joe's words.

"Next time, just grasp the ring. Don't put your hand through," he said. "I'll block you." Jute nodded.

It wasn't long before the boat shuddered, engines quiet. "Lock up the men," came the loathed familiar cry.

Jute looked at Joe who shut one eye. Jute reached his left hand toward the ring and grasped the metal, letting his arm hang slack as the chain was tightened.

"Drats," muttered Joe.

Then instead of calling, "All's clear," up the ladder as he usually did, he knocked into the lamp. It crashed off its metal hook and went out, leaving shadows from the open furnace flickering on the walls of the hold.

"Lights out," Joe bellowed.

A junior officer scurried down the ladder. Joe's foot barred the bottom, sending the man sprawling, cursing in the dark. Now, thought Jute, my only chance is now! Joe was helping the officer to his feet. In the dark confusion Jute slipped up the ladder. The stokers, fastened, said nothing, if they saw him go.

The junior officer struck Joe heavy blows about his face and shoulders. "Clumsy fool. You could have set the boat ablaze! Pick up that lamp and set to rights!"

Jute could still hear his hoarse angry voice as he peered around the unfamiliar deck. Over the side he thought.

## CHAPTER ELEVEN

### Cincinnati

Once above board, Jute watched the hived activity as the boat prepared for another overnight portside stay. Everywhere someone carried a box, coil of rope, or piece of luggage.

He stayed in the shadow of the cabin, spying out the anchor line piercing the boat's side, creeping near. Giving a furtive glance behind, to make certain no one was watching, he scissored his legs over the railing, sliding down the chain into the water. Heading downstream swimming hard, vision blurred, shoulders aching, he pushed the water behind him without a backward glance toward Susu or the Isle of Green.

Luke'd told Jute on shore they'd be parted only a short time. Could they really meet in the city as promised once the boat docked proper? In such a big place — everything strange?

Jute swam until he could no longer see the dark shape of houses clustered on the shore. Soon the brush along the river was unbroken by clearings. Turning toward the bank, he pulled himself up on a small patch of river mud where he lay shivering, gasping for breath, belly down like a dead flounder. Once his breath came even, he remembered he could still be seen by river boats come light and dragged back aboard ship to stoke coal, chained at every port. He scuttled part way up the bank, until, hidden in the thorny undergrowth, he slept through day till dark. What was ahead was too heavy for him to worry on another day without food.

Once awake worries of Susu came back all in a rush. Alone with a white family, what could she do here? Who'd help if Luke's scheme slipped wrong? The fear of that thought twisted his skull, knotted his stomach.

Should've let her keep her bits and pieces, but they'd 've stuck out, bumps hidden under the tight dress. Her hands 'd show off dark if she played some on the boat. Tears in her eyes though moved even Bessie's practical heart. She'd sewed the corn cob doll inside the extra space high in the small dark bonnet, warning Susu, "Don't take this out none till back with our own folk, hear?"

All that was left from home, Jute thought. The kettle, warm clothes and Momma's shawl still back in the barn.

The river cut deep here. Jute had to hang on to branches, inching himself up still further, climbing hand over hand, until it was level atop the bank.

A well worn road, deep rutted in spots, ran along the cliff. Jute followed it back toward the city, walking easy in the early evening river breeze. The clatter of horses with a buggy behind gave him warning to duck again. Wasn't enough to wait for dark with folks nearby. It had to be late, too. Hidden again, the hours slugged by. Jute was impatient to find Susu in the place Big Joe'd described so clear. He hadn't really worried on it till he left the ship.

"Keep along the river edge — soon the road's paved with stones," Joe'd said low, as they worked side by side near the furnace's blasting glare. T'other side of the high-toned part, clear through town, a small white building with some paint wore off and a cross atop where the road forks — our folks' church. Back door's always unlatched, floor covered with straw. Brush it away an' lift up the ring in the trap. Down cellar, jest wait, somebody'll come when the way's clear. Might be a heap o' others scattin. "Keep still 'till help shows."

Jute remembered those words as he sat itching to be on. Still hiding, but closer. Down the river closer, my own people helping now!

When he thought the small hours of the night had come, he started out once more in the direction of the city glimpsed from the Isle of Green. The excitement of what lay ahead sharpened his senses. Every sound and smell told him of the strange land approaching, a city bigger than Jute'd ever known.

The houses piled near on top of each other heading into town. Some had a short patch of stubble out front; others boasted a fence of black metal or an ornamental gate. Anywhere there might be someone peeping out between the curtain.

Jute swaggered like he had a right to be there, on that open road leading into Cincinnati. Mayhap if he was watched, it would be better to look at home. Once a dog gave him a start, bounding out with a yelp as if expecting someone else. He soon gave up the chase and slunk home as if the mistake had been his.

The rutted track became stones, cobbled rough and wide, straight along the shore. Some of the buildings were stores made of brick, two floors high! Night sights of the city closed in on him; trash bins, piled full, lined narrow walkways; a mangy cat picked his way atop a high board fence. The smell of burned out cook stoves, mixed with the muddy odor of the river nearby. He met nobody. The night was black.

By the pier, the huge shape of the Isle of Green tied up near, other boats loomed before him. He'd almost reached the right place. Houses got smaller again, less grand — almost a shanty town. He spied the white building with a wooden cross on top, a wooden sign out front. It sent his heart apounding. He'd found it!

\* \* \*

All dressed and ready to leave the boat, Susu followed Mrs. Templeton back down the corridor that morning. She no longer felt every line of the close fitting dress. The gray gloves still cramped her fingers, and the hat pins keeping her bonnet on the smoothed mass of her hair jammed sharply as before into her head. It made her feel better knowing her doll was there too. She looked around her through the shielding veil. More sure-footed, she no longer worried that her feet would slide out from underneath her at every step.

"Stay near me," Mrs. Templeton reminded her once on deck. The danger that they'd be separated by other people in the crush was real. Many playing children, dodging around the busy workers, distracted her from the single purpose—remaining close to this lady.

Where was Jute? She missed that straight back, that familiar cat walk, as he picked his way, always careful. Jute! Susu want to run to him and go where he was going, together as they had always been before. She didn't know she'd miss him so until she was mixed with strangers, going the other way without a backward glance to the ship or sign that she had kin.

Mrs. Templeton'd told her before they'd ever seen this ship that she would have to leave Jute for awhile. Had to leave him here. She must pretend she had no one, till they reached a safe place in the city. Now the time had come to play this game.

It seemed hours until, the gangplank lowered, they walked ashore with the others. Amidst all the talking people, Susu saw John Templeton with some men, watching the coffin being lowered from the hold. It landed with a jarring bump on the ground. It'd be worse to be in a coffin. Susu thought on Nate.

"My son will see to our bags when he hires a wagon for Mr. Templeton, God rest his Soul," said Mrs. Templeton, as much for anyone who cared to hear as for Susu to understand. Sweeping her long black skirt into one gloved hand, she began to pick her way across the cobble-stone street, up the hill toward town. She shook her head at a carriage standing there for hire, turning instead toward the busiest street lined with stores. The largest store filled a city block. Handsome stone steps led up from the street. A large plate glass window displayed all kinds of wares.

"Come along child. We must prepare for the funeral and our stay in Cincinnati."

Inside, the store smelled of tobacco, camphor, and new clothes. Fancy foods in shining jars lined one side, clothing of all sizes, the other. A long counter ran down the middle, heaped with yards of ribbon, lace, and more fine stuffs than Susu had ever seen. Mrs. Templeton moved slowly toward the rear of the store lightly fingering things as she went. Susu followed. She wanted to take off the prickly hat and dark veil that made it hard to see here out of the sun.

Two ladies, buying prunes by the pound, turned their eyes from the large scale to watch their progress. Turning back, they lowered their voices so Susu couldn't hear what they said. Could they tell she wasn't a white girl? Could they see her face behind the veil? Did they know she didn't belong in this store with all its fine things and with Mrs. Templeton? Their purchases finished, the women bustled out. A bell tinkled as they left. Now there was only a man in a white shirt with striped arm bands polishing up the counter with a soft yellow cloth. It was hard to see.

Mrs. Templeton turned. Still holding Susu's hand, she approached the man directly.

"Your shipment, Mr. Pembroke," she said, "arrived this morning on the Isle of Green. More to come by wagon."

"Many thanks," he answered. He'd taken out a long gray book and was figuring a column of numbers on one page. Without stopping his addition, he nodded toward an archway behind him, curtained in a dark, red, heavy material. Was Jute in there, Susu wondered?

Mrs. Templeton led Susu behind the curtain. She freed her hand from the clinging fingers in the soft gray gloves, pushing ahead expectantly. No one was there. She shuffled her feet and waited for Mrs. Templeton to tell her what to do.

"You'll be all right here, child. Do as you're told. Someone will bring you to your brother. I'd be spotted down there at the church."

She stopped a minute as if, feeling Susu's many questions, she wanted to stay and answer them one by one. Where? When? How? tumbled in Susu's mind. But Mrs. Templeton was gone, only the curtain swaying to show that she'd been there.

The room was filled with a jumbled mass of boxes, opened, wares yet unsorted. In the corner sat an old velvet chair, tattered stuffing showing at the corners, and a small stove, its belly glowing, a kettle set back to simmer.

Susu stood for a while looking about her, before crossing to the worn chair. She tried to perch on the edge of the seat but soon slipped back into its downy lap and cuddled there so warm she was almost asleep when the outside door opened.

"Lawd, what you doing there? I might've missed you all curled up in Mr. Pembroke's chair."

Susu jumped up, facing a tall, dark woman in a black figured dress, neatly covered by a long white apron that matched the turban on her head. She had smooth dark skin and almond eyes that sparkled when she spoke. The woman turned Susu round and round. Her chin jutted out. She laid a finger beside her cheek, as if to give approval to what she saw.

"My, ain't that a rig," she laughed at last, "and not a speck of you showing through. We'll fix all that. You can come out in the sunshine now, honey."

Susu stood there, unflinching, while the woman removed all but the long white drawers and the new shoes and stockings.

"Seems a shame," muttered the woman to herself, as she took a large pair of shears from the table and cut the lace flounce from the bottom of the drawers. The hat hurt Susu when the woman pulled it free. Some of the pins stayed in her head. She slipped a dress on Susu made of the same black print as her own. Like Susu's own dress from home, it had a neckhole and sleeves, no tight hooks up the back. It smelled clean, like linens dried in the sun.

"You look just fine to come to church with me." said the woman. She went into the store, leaving Susu behind, hearing muffled tones of Mr. Pembroke's voice and the big woman's hushed answers. When she returned, she gave Susu a little push toward a street door leading directly from the small back room.

Susu hung back, pointing to her bonnet. "No place for that where you be going," said the woman. "My dolly," said Susu, its importance giving her courage. The woman looked where she pointed, spying the clever device. She quickly ripped Bessie's stitches and returned the precious keepsake. It fitted Susu's hand — a loved one returned.

Once outside, Susu felt freer to look around. She walked straight on. She had to keep up with the tall woman's striding pace.

The people they passed seemed bent on errands of their own and didn't spare a glance for the large turbaned Negro woman or the little girl at her side. Soon they reached the church and entered by the wide front door.

"My name's Mindrah. My man sweeps up here nights," said the woman. "We live out back. No one pays no mind to my comings. We don't put a light on, though, until a spell after new folks arrive, lest anyone atrailing spots they don't come out again," she said to Susu.

She picked up a broom leaning near the back door and swept the straw away from the trap cut in the floor. Susu was frightened of the black pit yawning at her feet.

"I'm staying here. Go on, girl. You'll be all right," said the woman. "There's company down there till your brother shows, and I'll be back with supper and a light a'fore long."

Susu groped down the stairs, one unwilling foot after the other, the only sound the steady rasping breathing of a sick babe.

"Over here, child," said a deep voice. A hand led her to a bench along the wall. She wedged in between two bodies as slight as her own. Her eyes slowly grew accustomed to the dark. She could see about a dozen shapes ranged around the walls. The two next to her were children, one smaller and one almost her own size. Susu scanned each shadow around the room for Jute's familiar form. He wasn't there!

Sometimes a hushed voice spoke with long spells of listening in between.

"Two more to come," one voice said.

"We're to go by rail from here," whispered another.

"Never did trust no train riding. Too easy to get stopped and spotted," said a third.

"What's your name?"

It took Susu a while to figure out the last question was aimed at her from the girl whose shoulder, so close, was touching her own.

"Susu," she answered.

Susu'd gotten used to sitting on the hard bench. She learned that one girl's name was Leah, the smaller one Missy. But always she couldn't stop thinking, what if Jute never comes? The woman near Susu was having trouble keeping the sick one from fretting too loud.

"Been ailing since we started," volunteered Leah, the infant's older sister. The baby quit sucking on the breast thrust against her protesting mouth and whimpered louder.

Suddenly the trap lifted. Jute stood outlined in the lighter gloom of the church above.

\* \* \*

Jute had followed an alley round back to a door, white as the cross, set in the rear of the building. It had a bolt and padlock, both open. He inched the door ajar, no squeak here. Well-oiled hinges led him inside. There was a stuffy smell of straw and the lingering odor of many people packed together. He could almost see the congregation singing, stomping, and praying of a Sunday, touching shoulders on the hard black benches, barely visible in the now silent church.

Jute wasted no time. The door shut, he knelt and brushed the straw aside, 'till the outline of a trap door was clear to his groping hand. It pulled up easy, but Jute wondered about the straw above. Who'd scatter it back over the cracks? The half light of the church gave way to total darkness below. He braced the wet stone wall, feeling with his feet for each step. He felt but did not see the presence of many people waiting in the dark. Stifling, stale air reached out at him. He heard the shallow breathing of people trying to be quiet. He felt the press of bodies in the cellar. The trap door closed above him, cutting off that route for escape.

Panic almost sent Jute racing back up those steps. Who was waiting here? How could he know they were friends? Might be a heap of folks, Joe'd said, but who? His eyes tried to pick out faces in the dark. One shape broke away from the rest.

Susu rushed toward him, butting her sharp chin into his stomach as he reached the bottom step, her bony arms tangled around his waist.

"Jute, Jute," she repeated, burying her head above his knotted belt. She leeched on to him.

Jute's heart shifted.

"Susu," he whispered, tousling the hair so matted down by pins. "Susu."

## CHAPTER TWELVE

## The Train

It wasn't long after Jute arrived in the cellar that Mindrah came back bringing food. She left again, leaving two short fat candles sputtering in a holder set on the floor. With the light, women started talking together. Three mothers, young children huddled near, worried about the sick infant.

"Try a sugar tit," said one, dipping a corner of her kerchief into the molasses left over from the grits supper. It dribbled unnoticed on the hot cheek, puffed little mouth now gasping for air.

"She needs root tea ladled down her gullet. I know jest how to find the right fixing, skin the roots till the new green parts show an' mix 'em to a fine brew."

"Might help her breathe," joined another.

The wailing child's mother bent over the tiny form, mopping the small beaded forehead. Soon, the cries, grown weaker, only whimpers, shuddered the tiny form as the night crawled by.

"Had a mighty bumpy ride, but didn't have to swim," said a low voice close to Jute's ear. Turning, he recognized the shiny cropped head of Nate.

"When do we move on?" Jute asked. He felt crowded by the many new faces. Disliked the press of bodies in the airless room, ready to be going—now!

Learning from the men he couldn't just, 'float up river to Canada,' he'd been listening to tales of the train ahead. How'd he get so mixed up—river didn't even go in that direction so far.

"We go by rail. Sposed to be a stock car coming through. Won't be here till past midnight," said Nate.

There was a stir in the corner near the woman with the sick child, a low muffled cry, stifled almost at once. Silently now, the mother rocked her child. The baby coughed once, a strangled sound within the cradling arms. Then no more. The infant's mother bent over the little body, rubbing the small chest and arms repeatedly to no avail. Quiet pushed at the walls of the crowded cellar.

The appaling hush was more frightening than the labored painful breathing had been. Several women tried to revive the child, working the little arms up and down, patting the small one's back harder, as if the last strangling cough lodged in the tiny throat could be shook out and breathing air rushed in. They gave up after a bit and handed the child back to its grieving mother.

Jute knew the baby'd died. No one needed to be told. The mother's face, too worn for tears, showed grief in every line. One woman took the small body and wrapped it in an underskirt hastily torn off for the purpose.

Jest like Momma, Susu's heart hammered, jest like Momma.

After a hubbub of indecision, one man said, "Bury the mite here. We can't tote her along where we're going; wouldn't be right."

The small bundle was gently placed in a hole scooped in the hard dirt with tin plates and mugs, later, filled in, patted back by many hands.

All wishing we could do more, thought Jute. Could save a life that should've grown. Mindrah's husband, Tim, brought back a board, the name and date still tacky with new paint.

"Have to bury this, too." he said. The board was laid under a last layer of earth on top of the tiny form. Tim heaped extra dirt in a pail to carry out later.

"Preacher would've come," he said, "but he's sitting up with old Mrs. Hill again."

To leave now would be suspicious. So late at night.

"We'll do the best we can right here. Reckon the Lord'll forgive our mistakes," said an old man Jute'd noticed before, sitting quiet in a corner, fingering a worn hat in work-creased hands. He'd said nothing till now, his voice a brittle rasp like dry leaves scratching against a stone wall. He got up tall, though still bent when standing, his face the color of scorched paper not quite burned, framed by grizzled white hair. His knotted fingers clutched the hat to his breast as he bent at the foot of the tiny grave, waiting.

All the others followed his lead, ringed round the newly patted earth. Even children, big eyed, quiet, waited for him to speak.

Jute noticed tears in Susu's eyes. Tears for the babe she'd never known. Made her look older somehow and sad, kneeling there next to a girl could be the dead'uns sister.

"'Scuse us, Lord, if these ain't proper words for burying," began the old man. "There's no real preacher here. We ask you kindly to take this small soul to your bosom. She didn't make it to Freedom, but she didn't die bondsman neither. In your house, Lord, she'll grow up and serve without chains an' sing in the sunshine of your Heaven forever. Bring her mother more little'ns to fill her heart. An' help lead us all to Freedom 'fore we join you in the Promised Land. Amen."

"Amen," answered the kneeling people.

Amen, echoed Jute's heart, but he spat out the word like a curse. What were they all doing here, hats in hand, with a dead'un, buried in a cellar at night, where the light of day wouldn't ever reach till glory come and hallelujah? Couldn've been Susu buried there like Momma with no doctor. Not even any of the root tea the women know how to make from their Grannies. Still kneeling, he hit the earth with his fist, its sound only a muffled thud. The old man looked up, noticing Jute's grim anger 'midst the sorrowing mourners.

"We'll move on, boy. 'Fore morning we'll move on."

His hand on Jute's shoulder brought comfort, an unexpected bond. Someone did know how he felt.

\* \* \*

They were all ready to leave that place when Tim came back down the stone stair. Some had bundles tied together close by their feet. Jute's gear, lugged across mountains, abandoned now. Don't miss it none, he thought — yet. Might come in handy up ahead. Jute could hear the train throbbing when the trap door lifted.

"One, then wait a beat," cautioned Tim. "Cut across the fields behind our cabin to the track. The yards are up ahead. Sheep to be loaded are in the pen on this side. Duck no higher than a sheep's back, 'an keeps your head down."

When Jute's turn came, his long legs reached the field's edge quickly. Bent low, he noticed patchy moonlight above. The bleating of sheep in the pen almost covered the grating train, as it stopped at the yard up ahead. The stock car, empty, even with the pen, was shaking a little, as if eager to start again.

"Climb over the top," Tim said. "Lie down foots to heads and stay flat."

Jute jostled around to get next to Susu before they climbed over the top rail. Lying flat, he pressed into her side. Susu'd come far. She didn't look at him like it was all his fault no more, always like she'd rather be home, comfortable, sleeping nights.

Susu wiped her sleeve against a tear-stained face and tried to lie quiet next to Jute. Foots to heads, the man'd said. She lined herself up even with Jute's bare feet, her shoes hardly reaching above his waist. A layer of stiff hay was spread over the people. Next to her was the little girl just her size. Leah, she'd called herself back in the cellar before the baby died. Spreading her fingers, she could reach Leah's hand and clasp it. She didn't dare hold on to Jute. He'd shake her away sure. The hay piled on top of the people was scratchy, sharp. Instead she hugged her loved doll close.

What would the ride be like? Susu'd never been on a real train. Some men hustled on the stock car, let down a ramp for sheep, first putting planks up over the hay. They nailed them on with loud, jarring strokes. Susu flinched at the hammering above her head. Seemed the men would miss and hit her. The patform ready, next more hay and the sheep, clattering on horny feet, their shifting weight a constant tapping overhead. The side ramp was hauled up. The rattling train, after a few false starts backwards, began chugging, slowly ahead, around a bend and through the freight yard into open country beyond.

Susu didn't like the train. Wheels, so close below her, ground sharp, tearing at her ears. Stomping sheep above let out an awful stink. Sometimes their droppings rolled through open planks, sifting on people, mingling with the dust of the dry road bed and thorny hay. Susu learned to squinch her eyes tight to keep out the grit that made it hard to see. She squeezed Leah's hand and felt her squeeze back. Both, frightened of the noise and speed, the little girls hung on, wondering when it would end.

She slept a while, jerking awake with fright whenever the train stopped. Dinner seemed a long time back. Grits in the cellar. Nothing ahead was sure. Her mouth salty, parched, with a thirst there was no way to quench, bad as riding in a coffin, thought Susu.

On the Isle of Green she'd had a bed and little pieces of soft bread with stuff gluing it together, and hot tea. Her mouth puckered remembering. Through the veil she'd seen water and all the people. Here she could see nothing. She licked her lips, but it just made them drier, cracked and peeling. She closed her mouth quick against the sheep dung and spiky stalks.

The train stopped longer than before.

"We're getting out," Susu whispered to Leah, aching to sit up.

"Shut," whispered Jute.

Angry voices up ahead and a lantern's fractured glow through the wide plank sides made Susu hold her breath.

"You've no call to stop this train," one man shouted.

"Here's searching papers. We've reason to believe someone's harboring Nathaniel Tompkins, called Nate, lawful property of William Lyons, Carolina. We've traced him far as Cincinnati. This here train's one way out of the city."

"You'll be later yet if we have to bring the constable and issue warrants and the like," chimed in a third man stronger than the others.

The voices were muffled by the clanking open of rusted siding doors as cars ahead were searched.

Still talking loud, men jumped onto the stock car.

"Why's this car higher than the others?"

"We're one car short this trip. Had to put fodder underneath." The answer sounded smooth to the listening ears straining below. People who had so much to lose hung suspended, waiting for the reply.

"We'll just have to take these boards off and have a look."

"Suit yourself, but hurry. I've not all day to stop here, and this not even a junction. Wish to Hell you'd keep hold of your property and not keep letting it slip off to bother other people's work. Now mind, each plank'll have to be nailed back proper. Can't have the boards sliding—break a lamb's foot. They only pays me for the live ones I deliver."

"Christ almighty! You mean they's all nailed down?"

"You can see the fodder down there. Here, stick your sword through."

"Don't carry no sword. Think I'm a blooming general or something?"

"All right, let's move on. We'll see what you've got in the next car. We ain't got time to mess with hammering stuff. I'm ready to leave this stink hole."

The men tromped out, opening the last car, a closed one with a door that sounded hard to budge.

"Hanging Twerps, you can give me a hand here." The last words they heard the patrollers say, as the voices moved away into the night, "we'll ketch up with him yet."

Later, the train clanked. Susu forgot she was hungry and thirsty and that the hay stuck into her face. They hadn't taken off the planks! Seemed no one breathed yet, though the train inched forward slowly.

It was still dark when they stopped again. This time she didn't squeeze Leah's hand, waiting for the men to come back. Bolts on the side ramp slid open, and it was lowered once more. The sheep, led off, skittered down the ramp as eager to be free as the people cooped below. Nails wrenched loose, groaned creaking as boards were pulled back leaving an opening three feet wide. A round dark face leaned over, helping as each section was removed. A meaty hand brushed away straw cover and helped ease cramped bones to sitting, then standing positions. Susu looked back at Jute.

"Go on," he said. "Go on out." The message given to each one was the same.

"Run cross the field to that empty depot up next to the track, 'an go on in."

Susu looked back once more at Jute just shaking free the straw and climbing out. She ran forward on stiff legs across a field too dark to see. Running, her feet plunked heavily down one after the other, as if they didn't belong to her. Suddenly she pitched forward in the semi-dark, a searing pain, a crack, then nothing.

## CHAPTER THIRTEEN

## The Choice

Watching others run toward the empty depot in mottled moonlight, Jute saw Susu pitch forward and disappear in the high grass. He cleared the bars of the stock car with one jump, landing free of the cindered road bed. He crossed the field quickly, weeds tugging his ankles. Susu was lying in a crumpled heap, one leg twisted to the side, a jagged point of bone protruding below her knee, blood pooling dark on her torn stockings. Gathered in his arms, she weighed little more than the kettle and bundle of clothing he'd lugged so far.

The door of the depot swung back as he approached. Other stragglers pushed in behind Jute till everyone from the church was again huddled under one roof. In the silvered light sifting through large broken windows, Leah was the first to notice Jute carrying Susu, her stillness and the stain spreading down to her shoes.

"What's happened?" she gasped, tugging at Jute's arm. "Is she dead?"

Jute knocked her hand away. Moving through the gathering crowd, he laid Susu on the depot bench.

Women nudged him back as they bent over the little girl. Tearing loose the white cloth of her long drawers, they picked the frayed stockings away from the splintered bone. Susu's head began to move from side to side on the rough wooden planks of the bench. She made a slight gasping sound before opening her eyes, frightened, wide, filling with tears, darting, till they fastened on Jute's face.

"We'll bind it up with strips of her petticoat to help the bones knit together," said one woman, beginning to shred the underskirt Susu'd worn on the Isle of Green.

Shapes clouded Jute's head: Momma dying, buried on a farm he'd never pass again. At night, with only strangers around, none of the home folks she loved nearby. Last night the baby, whose name he didn't know, laid under the dirt floor of a moldy church cellar.

"No," he said. "She'll be doctored right before we moves her. Doctored like white folks back home."

Nate stepped through the crowd of women, bending over Susu.

"We're latching on tonight, son," Nate's voice was as determined, as Jute remembered when Nate'd stepped into the coffin and ordered the lid closed over him. "Lots of plans and scheming led us here. This next train's moving on to Detroit, then Canada. It has space for us and clothes and papers, too. Going straight through with guards, and guns. It won't be stopped. We don't have to ride under the sheep dung nailed in with the fodder no more. This train's to Canada, boy."

All the drive of Jute's long haul hammered in his throat. The pushing ahead over the mountains; scratching for food; Snake Island and the men's voices hallooing over the water; dock workers plotting to turn him in for fifty dollars reward; the shoving, hauling, dragging Susu to get her here; this man telling him at last freedom was a sure thing, a plum ripe for the picking. He swallowed it all back.

"Can't help that," he said. "She'll be doctored right."

"Someone would have to set out to haul a doctor from his bed. If'n there is one, an' it not even daybreak," said Nate, shaking his head doubtfully.

"I'll go," said Jute. He leaned over Susu once more. Moaning now, she was thrashing on the hard wood. Teeth biting back blood till she fainted against the pain.

"I'll be back soon." He grasped Leah's wrist. "Don't leave her. Promise!"

Leah nooded her small head, teeth clattering together in fright at his sudden hard touch and the husky sharpness of his command.

Nate pulled him back with a stopping hand. "If the train arrives, Leah will have to go. Her mother's lost one child this trip. She'll leave," said Nate. "Stay. Put Susu on the train. Her leg's bad broke, sure, but even bad legs've mended before. Stay with us, Jute!"

Jute held himself stiff against Nate's pleas, thinking, another man pushing me around, telling me where to step, but this man knew what Jute wanted. He wanted it himself, enough to ride in a coffin, jouncing a long wagon's ride to the river and staying closed up in the dark hold of a boat. Jute could almost smell freedom — close now!

He shook his head, the stubborn set of his mouth told the others what he'd say. "I'll fetch the doctor. There may still be time to do both."

Jute turned at the door. "Where's this place at?" he asked.

"Up ahead's Xenia," said the old man who'd preached the cellar funeral. "Should find a doctor there. The main road crosses the tracks up ahead below the next dip. Jim said we could spot the roof of the new brick depot closer to town. Course, the doctor mightn't be colored."

Jute flung out into the night. All them mountains an' rivers crossed, an' she steps into a grounding hole here, he raged to himself.

His fists pumped against his pounding legs. He didn't try to walk quietly. Gravel filled ruts along the hard mud-packed road. Some houses heading toward town began to show lamps turned on in kitchens along the way. Jute studied the crossroads briefly and took the turn that looked as if it headed into town, more wagon ruts in the dried mud.

One could be the doctor's. No way to tell, not even a name to search out, he thought.

Finally, with speed and thoughts of Susu moaning on that bench pushing at him, he turned, almost running up one path to the back door of a large brick house. A lamp was lit somewhere within. Somebody's up in here. He banged his fist against a heavy green door.

It seemed an age before the bolt was drawn and a woman in a white cap peeped out, wary, on guard, chain drawn.

"Need a doctor back there." Jute pointed in the direction he'd come. His voice, unused to talk and out of breath, came harsh, louder than he meant.

"A wreck, a train wreck?" asked the woman, curious. Interest kindled, she opened the door a bit further.

Jute thought fast. Mustn't startle her none. He realized for the first time the sight he made appearing sudden, ragged, out of breath.

"No'm," he replied, forcing a hated meek tone of voice. "Just a little girl. Her leg's broke bad. Needs a doctor to set it straight. Where would he be at? Please."

"Oh," the woman sounded disappointed somehow. She's broken her leg has she? Where's she living? Whose little girl is it?"

Jute felt trapped. He wanted to tear the words from her and run. His need for speed to find a doctor and get the job done before the train arrived forced him to press on. How long would she stand there yammering at him?

"She's bad, miss. Got to get the doctor quick. Losing blood an' all," he answered, ignoring her questions.

"Oh yes, of course," said the woman. "Dr. Sammison should be at home this time of day, if Mrs. Little hasn't had her baby in the night or the Lydesser twins aren't down with the croup."

She seemed about to go on when Jute broke in.

"Where's he at?"

"Round the next corner. Lives by himself since his sister died, with just a day woman to do for him and a hired hand. A yellow house with a fence around it and yews each side of the door. Name plate's out front. Dr. Sammison. S-a-m-m-i..."

But Jute'd turned and was running toward the street, leaving her standing there, lamp in hand. She muttered, shaking her head as she shut and bolted the door against the early chill.

From the doctor's gate, four strides took Jute to the front door. He raised a tarnished knocker. No lights on here. Jute knocked twice more before the doctor came. A short man, knotting a plum-colored dressing gown around his heavy middle, he pulled Jute inside and closed the door.

Jute hadn't wondered "what if he won't come?" till now. Hadn't thought beyond his need to find the man to set the bone. Now he feared plenty. What could he do if the white doctor had a mind to turn him in, to turn them all in? He'd risked all the careful plans of Nate and the others with his stubborn need to have Susu doctored proper. He'd have to sell the idea to this man quick before the train passed them by.

"Catch your breath, boy," said Dr. Sammison.

Standing in the dim hall, Jute realized he'd been panting and fought for control while sorting out the proper words. The doctor had a mottled, red face. His thick nose showed purple veins. White whiskers winged out each cheek. He wiped some pinch spectacles on a crumpled white handkerchief before snapping them on his nose with a sharp click.

"Go on," he said to Jute. "Tell me what's wrong. Who needs fixing this time of morning?"

"My sister's broke her leg," said Jute. "Stepped in a hole or something down by the old depot. Bone's snapped clear through."

Jute took a chance. His feel for people hadn't failed him yet.

"But we have to go on tonight," he said. "There's supposed to be a train. We've got to be on that train, doctor, but Susu's leg's bad. Will you help?

Jute heard the begging, crawling tone in his own voice and didn't care. If only this man would come with him now, quick!

"More of Reverend Bartlett's work, I'll be bound," mused the doctor. "Folks come through here regular," he said.

"Some of the town's not unfriendly to your cause. Last spring a pair of patrollers chasing after a slave family was driven back down the main street by a hooting mob throwing stones. They threatened to get the law and come back, but they never showed up here again. Yep, Xenia's got her heart set 'agin seceders. Not like a few years back. Stay here. I'll get dressed. We'll see how bad off she is."

Jute, relieved, wanted to pull the man outside. Dressed! How long would that take? He paced the small front hall, listening to the doctor's footsteps in the bed chamber overhead. He could smell the stuffy closed house, mixed with the herbs and medicines doctors use. His eyes began to smart, realizing he smelled too, of sweat, dung, fear.

Jute thought he could hear the train clacking in the distance, going off and leaving him behind. They may be friendly here, but Ohio wasn't no freedom land. He'd said there was patrollers! Not always driven off. Just one time they'd tell about. What about the other times when there wasn't no mob on Main Street? Jute remembered the men on the train asking after Nate by name. He wasn't safe yet. He'd no freedom papers or passes and none to give him any.

Dr. Sammison returned fully dressed in a black waistcoat and jacket, white whiskers pulled down, didn't stand out so far to the side. He still didn't seem ready to go. Drawing a heavy gold watch on a chain, he glanced up at the standing clock in the hall and wound the watch in a measured way before mentioning his bag. He went through a curtained doorway at the back of the house. Jute glimpsed rows of shelves and bottles when the curtain parted. The doctor beckoned him through. They left by the rear door close to the barn.

"My hired hand's gone," said the doctor, leading a stout bay from his stall. "Hold his head while I fasten these straps."

He backed his horse between the buggy's shafts. Jute held the bridle while the buggy was hitched in place. Then, clucking his horse out of the barn, the doctor lumbered up onto the high black seat. He tapped a spot beside him, and Jute, too, clambered into place.

"You're better outdoors he said to Jute." Fanning his hat in front of his nose.

At last things seemed to move a proper pace as the horse's footsteps echoed on the empty road, retracting Jute's way back to Susu. The doctor's solid shape was reassuring. For the first time Jute allowed himself to hope. He'd have heard the train if it'd come. Once Susu's leg was fixed, they could be on their way with the others headed north.

All was quiet when the buggy turned into the depot. Jute couldn't tell if people were still inside, and for a heart beat he thought they'd all gone. The doctor entered first.

Everything was as before, some men resting on the floor, backs braced against the wall. The children clustered together, or near their mothers. Susu on the bench, her face pinched with pain and crying. New tears joined old, pooled on her face. A woman bent over her, trying to comfort, with nothing to ease the pain. That awful leg was propped up, the bleeding caked, dry, the bone still showing through purpling skin.

Dr. Sammison didn't stop to look about him. He moved to Susu's side and laid a rounded soft-looking white hand on her head. No one broke the heavy silence as his hand moved down to probe the wound. Susu cried out, the sharp shriek pathetic, lonely, making Jute's skin crawl with wishing it was his leg broke and hurting.

"It must be set before she's moved," said the doctor, unbuttoning his waistcoat. He removed his jacket carefully, folding it and the vest back to fore. He placed them on the bench near Susu's head. Slowly he unfastened the still white cuffs of his striped shirt, until his plump pink arms were bared to the elbows. "That open wound might fester."

He sent a man near the door for a lantern in his rig. "Light it and hold it steady," he said.

Opening his bag he drew out two green bottles, four smooth flat slats of yellow wood and a heavy roll of bandage fraying at the ends. The people watched as he lined these things up close to his jacket on the bench beyond Susu's head.

"I'll need some help," he said. "No hysterical types, neither. You there, you and you." He pointed a stubby finger at Leah's mother, Nate, and a tall man next to him who could have been the woman's husband.

To Jute he said, "You hold her head and shoulders steady and give her a stiff drink of this before we start." He pulled a cork on one of the bottles and handed it across Susu's body to Jute. Susu's eyes grew dark and widened with fear.

"No, no," she moaned. "Don't let him touch me none."

"He'll fix you, child. He's got to touch you to make you well," said Leah's mother, her sad face remembering her child who'd had no doctor's care. Her voice soft, but firm, helped quell Susu's panic.

Jute put an arm beneath her sweaty, tangled hair to lift her head up to the neck of the green bottle. She gulped the bitter tasting brew. The doctor uncorked the other bottle. The sharp smell of raw alcohol made Jute's eyes smart, drowning out the dark odor of unwashed bodies.

The doctor swabbed his clean handkerchief with the liquid and laid it dripping on the wound. Susu shrieked again, eyes streaming as she tried to squirm out of his grasp.

"Now hold her steady while I set this back in place," said Dr. Sammison. Pulling at the twisted leg, he straightened it with more strength than his pudgy arms seemed to possess. Snapping out orders, like one used to being followed, he gave directions to Nate and the other man.

"Bring those splints here. Lay 'em flat and start at the end of the bandage. Leave a strip hanging. Wrap it up tight. No, not like that," he barked. "Two underneath and one on each side. Start rolling from the front and lay the strips even. Now, I'll finish."

The splints in place, he could stop holding the leg straight and finish binding the slats in place himself. He made a tidy job of tucking under and tying the loose ends.

Jute'd held Susu's thrashing body till she fainted, near the start, lying there unmoving, limp. He kept his hands on her bird-like shoulders. Would it be over before the train came?

"There," said Dr. Sammison, rolling down his sleeves at last. "She'll come round soon, don't worry. We'll take her to my place till a more permanent spot can be found. She'll need care for a spell yet. Can't put weight on that foot if she's not to be crippled for life. May be yet, of course, but with that splint she has a chance to grow straight come spring. Young'uns mend fast. If she doesn't walk. And if the fever doesn't get her. And then there's the open wound to worry about."

"Spring!" Jute burst with all the outrage he felt. "That train's due in tonight! Even now it's late." He glanced at the high window showing light and for the first time noticed the long night was really past.

"Move her that far on a train, and you'd lose her from fever and the loss of blood," said the doctor.

"I'll carry her," said Jute.

"Can't be done. She's not strong enough to stand the trip. Keep her here or lose her sure, " he repeated with more authority. "That's your choice!"

Jute looked to Nate for help, but Nate, running a hand over his glistening head, shrugged and looked down.

There was no choice. Jute's mouth set a bitter line. The doctor gathered up his things and snapped his bag shut. All his movin' to get here just to be cornered now.

"How'll we get her there?" asked Jute at last, voice flat. He didn't want to be around when the train arrived. I'm in as big a rush to get away as I was to get here a bit ago, he thought.

The doctor finished rolling down his sleeves and carefully buttoned the last button of his jacket. Jute's jaw worked, but he said nothing. Scooping Susu's still quiet form in his arms once more, he left the depot without a word. Leah shuffled, her mother wiped her eyes with the back of her hand, but no one spoke. The doll, caked with blood, lay under the bench, forgotten.

"Try not to jar that leg," the doctor said over his shoulder. He untied the horse and climbed into the high seat. Leaning over he gave Jute an elbow up. The doctor seemed about to topple from his high perch as he helped Jute settle Susu in the buggy.

The rig moved off, slower than before, Dr. Sammison guiding his horse around every hole. Numb with defeat, Jute rode beside the man, unseeing. Unshed sorrow for his plan, turned sour, spiked his eyes.

He'd lost his hired man, the doctor'd said earlier. Was he just dragged back to fill those shoes? Should he believe what he'd been told? Susu might have thrived in Canada or might die here. He'd never know. Caring seemed to fade.

All Jute's fighting strength drained.

You did what you had to do, like he'd been told before by men who never left their home place — men like Poppa.

## CHAPTER FOURTEEN

### A Man's Job

Susu opened her eyes and looked at the white painted ceiling. She dimly remembered Jute carrying her in earlier and laying her gently on the bare ticking of a mattress so hard her body barely made a dent. Only her head sunk into the soft pillow.

She looked around the small room. A low window with flowered curtains pulled shut didn't keep out the light of mid-day. A green painted chest was the only other piece of furniture crowded against the big iron bedstead.

Her leg hurt. The searing pain, dimly remembered from last night at the depot, now throbbing, a sharp ache that never left and made it hard to think of anything else. She tried to move, but the screeching pain came harder. She stopped and looked down at her leg. A bulky bandage with wooden slats at the ends seemed to be holding her prisoner on the high unmade bed.

Where was Jute? She remembered that he'd brought her here but left at once with a strange white man. Where was he now? And where was she?

Susu recollected her own bed, smelling of the sweet dry grasses she and Momma gathered every fall. The wind blew through the cabin winters, but on warm spring nights she could count the stars through the cracks. She missed those cracks and home with a crying need she blinked back.

Startled, she heard Jute's voice outside somewhere but couldn't reach the curtains to peek out. Willing that sharp agony away forever, it was enough to know he was still near.

The door opened and a woman stood at the foot of Susu's bed. Her figured dress stretched over her bulging bosom where a gold locket swung on a chain. Tousled hair, pulled back into a knot, was light brown, but to Susu she looked old, lined, and tired, until she smiled, showing strong yellow horse teeth and blue eyes, lightened, warm.

"There you are," she said. Doctor said I'd find you here. And without even a sheet or counterpane! I'm Clara Martin. Worked for Doctor long before Miss Millie died. You'll need some fixing up and tucking in and could use a good scrub too."

Susu winced.

Clara Martin looked down at the swaddled leg and dusty shoes stretched out on the bare bed. "Won't touch that leg" she said. "I'll be back."

She returned with folded bedding and a quilt over her arm. Pushing in the narrow space between the chest and bed, she laid her armload down and pushed the curtains back. Propping the window open with a stick lying there for that use, she poked her head out and called.

"You there, come in here."

Jute, almost as tall as the white-planked door, looked out of place as he stood waiting for Clara to speak.

"Carry your sister to the other room while I make up this bed," she said, "and be careful of that leg. Doctor said she shouldn't be jarred none."

Jute scooped Susu up once more. She bit her lip to keep from crying out as he placed her on another bed in the next room, used in the past for the hired girl. A small room just like the first, it differed only in having curtains of a smaller pattern.

"Dr. Sammison says he'll keep us both till your leg's well enough to walk on," said Jute. "I'm to work as hired hand for our keep." His voice was flat.

Susu almost asked about the train and Leah, but something about the way his toe tapped out a pattern on the foot of the iron bedstead kept her quiet. He swiped his hand across his face, ill at ease, about to say something else, but he turned to leave as sudden as he'd come.

Susu wanted to cry out for him to stay with her. She wanted to hold him hard, to sob out with pain how sorry she was he'd missed the train to freedom because of her and her busted leg. She swallowed, her eyes full with the crying need.

"Dr. Sammison'll have work for me to do," he said over his shoulder on his way out.

The woman came back with a bowl and pitcher of water and a nightgown, pure white with fancy tucks and stitches around the neck. She talked as she removed Susu's dirty dress, scrubbing her all over except for her bad leg with a cloth wrung out and dipped again and again into warm soapy water. No one'd ever washed her like that before. Clara Martin's voice almost put Susu to sleep with the soft stream of words and the washing. The gown felt cool and loose when she slipped it over Susu's head.

Doctor said you could wear Miss Millie's gown. It's a shake too big but should stay on if it's buttoned at the neck. She was a fine woman. Left me this locket when she died — real gold with her picture and Dr. Jim's. I'll let you hold it some time if you're careful of the little catch and the hinge at the back. They'd bend easy if they was to be treated rough."

She held up Susu's thick hair and sighed.

"We'll start on that another day. I expect you'll be here long enough. Where were you going, you and your brother all alone? Doctor told me nothing but to care for you while you're here. As if the house wasn't enough without a hired girl to help. I expect you're running, but where from? Where're you going in such a hurry that you broke your leg?"

Susu looked up startled, wakeful again. She'd no words for all that she and Jute'd done. People and places swirled through her mind with no beginning and no end to speak about.

"I dunno," she mumbled.

"You can tell me, child," said Clara Martin, but Susu said no more.

Clara Martin measured three spoonsful of strong stuff from a brown bottle for Susu. It burned clear down her chest till her eyes ran water.

Jute, summoned again, carried Susu back when her own room was ready. The freshly made bed felt cool and comfortable. Left alone, Susu fingered the patterns on the quilt, until, trying to forget the pain, she fell asleep.

\* \* \*

All October Susu watched changing fall colors barely visable outside the small window beyond the iron bedpost, through waves of pain. As autumn ripened, Jute came seldom, only some nights. Eyes, glittering with a hate she'd seen him turn on others, made her quake.

"Can't you move yet?" he asked once, slit lips barely moving, looking at her shattered leg, still pinned to the bed by bulk splints.

Susu flinched, unanswering, at the reproach. All her doing, stopping here, all her doing!

How long would Jute bide it 'fore taking off— leaving her to fend alone? She daren't ask. His blacking mood never left.

Would she ever walk? The questions singed her lips, unasked when the doctor came to change the dressing, inspect the wound, firmly rewrapping the whole. He never said.

The nightmare of it woke her, cold sweats on her brow, fright pushing pain into the dark unknown.

As November turned to full winter, Susu vowed to practice walking alone when all were asleep.

Despite the piercing ache she swung her legs over the edge of her bed one night, putting her weakened good foot on the small braided bedside rug.

The room tilted, sliding, clutched counterpane, rug and all. She landed with a dazed thud wedged half under the iron frame, unable to move.

Her first thoughts were of Jute. He'd leave now, sure. Especially if she'd damaged herself more.

Seemed a packet later the door opened.

"For heavens sake missy, where are you?" The doctor's voice rang from the far side of the bed.

"Here," Susu wavered.

"What a fix. Let's see if we can do this without rousing anyone else."

His practiced hands lifted her, inspecting for further damage before tucking her under warm quilts.

"I'll get you crutches if you're so blamed eager to start walking," he said holding the door handle before leaving, "on condition — no trying'em without Clara Martin's help."

Susu nodded. Crutches! Maybe.

"Doctor," she said lightly, her voice catching him again. "Don't tell Jute 'bout the crutches."

"All right, all right little missy." He chuckled.

Mightn't work, an' if not Jute'd be angered sure. She feared plenty and daren't hope.

Early the next day Clara Martin stood a pair of crutches in the corner of Susu's room.

"Can't help you none till my work's done." She said, noting Susu's impatience. "And Doctor says you're not to use'm alone. Don't need more bones broke."

First try, Susu despaired she'd ever catch the knack.

Her maimed leg, still weighted by splints, pulled over to one side with every move. Passage down the hall, slow, jerkey. Sticks swung forward, tippy. Her legs dragged behind, uneven tracks on the flowered hall carpet.

Sticking to it, she learned to master a turn, tracking back to her room again. Each day's practice improved her balance, speed. Clara Martin'd let her walk daily within sight as she bustled, making beds, dusting.

Susu'd flop back on her bed. Tuckered with the ache, panting, but happy too. Would Jute forgive the time gone by?

All fall Jute worked around the place, bedding down the horse at night, up again at dawn to light the fires. The fire inside him rising up so he couldn't talk or see the doctor without a trapped feeling choking him. Chips scattered by his flying ax. Work kept him from feeling cool October turning to November's chill. Splitting kindling, carrying water for the horse, polishing up the brass, spreading corn husks on the doctor's garden out back. Always something to do.

Lying on his bed nights staring, a white ceiling, he'd think. I've changed a brown ceiling for a white one. That's all! That's all! His big talk of Canada preached to Poppa, to anyone that'd listen to him, trying to make them leave before it was too late—worthless.

Stinking as manure at high noon. Poppa hadn't stirred till he'd been sold. Jute pushed ahead and ended slave as much as any, here in the North.

He'd chop harder, angry thoughts piling up. Once, working so, he didn't see the doctor come out of his back door, down toward the chopping block. Watching Jute raise the ax, waiting for his chance to speak. The wood finished, Jute leaned down to gather up an armful for the kitchen fire.

"Hitch up the buggy, Jute, and come along. I've been up near all night and have just one more stop before I quit for today. I'll doze a bit on the way home while you drive."

Jute turned sharply without even a nod to show he understood. He disappeared into the yellow carriage house, leaving the doctor staring over the garden hedge, thoughtfully tapping his gold watch against his palm.

"What's at you, lad?" he asked, later in the buggy.

Surprised, Jute stared ahead unanswering.

"I've watched you since you came," continued the doctor. "More'n two months of hard work you gave me, hard angry work. You know, a doctor gets to feel things, and I don't like living with that bare hatred of yours under my roof. Maybe that's the way it is where you come from, but hired hands come and go here, when it suits 'em, and none've turned snakes eyes on me before. What's eating at your soul, boy? The past? The train that come and left without you? More trains been by this way since and more'll come. You can be on one once your sister's healed proper."

Still Jute said nothing, the hopelessness of what he felt replacing for the first time the distrust he'd been feeding since the night he came. Wasn't this man trapped him here. He'd taken Susu on his own. No use trotting out what he felt. Freedom was a hollow word. Couldn't picture it no more'n the next thing. He'd been a boy when he let the glory of freedom dangle before him, dazzling him on. For what?

"What do you want?" The doctor pushed on. "What'd you want of Canada?"

They jangled on a spell, each busy with his own thoughts.

"A man's job," Jute spat out at last. "A man's job with a man's pay."

He'd never thought on it that way before he'd put it into words, but once said, it seemed no more'n right. The barge men with a bale of tobacco to split and sell. They'd be free no matter where they chose to live or work. Wages was what he needed to feel a man, wages and his choosin' where.

The doctor rode on without speaking until they reached his patient's house.

"Wait here. I'll be out shortly," he said.

What if I don't wait, thought Jute. Just clucked those horses on till the hell wind blew behind them. Would he be free then, with his own rig to drive? Jute knew the answer without telling it—new folks hunting him out fresh—and Susu always pulling him back.

"I've given it some thought. I think you're right, Jute," Dr. Sammison said on the way home.

Jute, driving now, kept the reins even in his hands, but pressed so tight the edges made a ridge on both palms.

"I'll turn my mind to it," the doctor continued. "A regular paying job. Probably not at my place. Susu can't walk yet, but she'll be well enough to move for the winter, say after Christmas, I'll think on it a while. Must be someone about needs a man's help."

Days went by, filled with familiar chores. No one had to tell Jute what to do. Soon his jubilance at finding an answer to the question in his heart began to dim again. When would he learn not to listen? Another soft lying white tongue saying what he'd wanted to hear. He worked

111

hard as before without even hate to drive him, like a man wound up and set to task. Nights he felt mean he stayed away from Susu. Unable to watch her cringe into the covers blaming herself, as he blamed her, for the slow healing bones. Dr. Sammison sent for him one evening. Clara Martin fetched him to the study. She had her hat pinned on and left by the front door as he went through the curtained doorway. Dr. Sammison sat behind a dark desk piled high with heavy books, an inkstand and a spindle with a pile of crumpled papers held captive by the silver spike. He rolled a long dark pen between his hands stroking his whiskers with its feathered tip. He looked up when Jute came in.

"I think I've found a place for you," he said. "Negro farmer up the road, building himself a mill to grind his corn, down on Jacoby Creek, near Goes. Got it framed in by now, but needs help with the finishing this winter, and the running when he's done, come spring. Tucked away some. Nobody should bother you there."

He gave a final pat to his whiskers.

Jute hooked his thumbs into his hemp belt, his weight even on both feet, determined not to be taken in by joy he'd felt before, only to have another obstacle thrown in his path. "There's pay?" he asked. His voice, steady, surprised him with its normal sound.

"Wilson Geer's not a poor man, but he's far from rich. I'll see," answered the doctor. "His master freed him when he died, leaving him a hundred dollars cash. He bought some land north of here a bit. He's done well raising corn, buying more land bit by bit since then. This idea of his now, of putting up a mill himself to grind his corn and his neighbors, is costing some. I told him you'd be wanting money, but we haven't talked of price or where you and Susu would live. I've arranged for you to meet him next time I go down his way."

He consulted a small leather book open on the desk. "I'll make it soon's I can — say next Wednesday once the holiday's out of the way."

Jute visited Susu on his way back to the connecting carriage house. Wedged into the small space beside her door was the table and chair the doctor'd had him carry from the attic some months before. Susu could sit on the chair, her leg propped up on the bed and work out lessons in a copybook. She sat there now, heavy shawl around her shoulders and the door open to tempt some warmth from the woodstove in the rooms beyond.

Mrs. Bartlett, the reverend's wife, spent some time these past months teaching Susu to write, cipher, and knit. Bending over the page, Susu's lips followed the sums she wrote. She worked alone days. Nights Jute wasn't too mad, she'd read to him from Sally's Garden of Flowers. Each story about another flower given a girl's name and manners. Didn't much hold his interest. Susu read aloud with halting phrases, sounding out unfamiliar hard words.

She couldn't tell what he thought, sitting there, a coiled spring till dusk drove him slamming off to his own dark bunk.

Tonight, he didn't wait for any story.

"Put that back a bit," he said as she reached for the dark green book with its gilt pansy etched on its cover. "I've news! Come Wednesday a week, I'm to meet a man about a job. A job with pay!" His voice deepened with pride, she'd not heard before. He looked to Susu for her reaction.

She waited with that calm he'd noticed of late, a quiet born of pain and patience. She's older, the thought drifting through his mind. The young, impatient, almost baby girl he'd dragged away from home was gone. She didn't ask about her place in his plan, but must be wondering some.

"Mrs. Martin and her husband will be moving in here to care for Dr. Sammison night and day with a new hired hand when one shows up. Down the road to Goes the doctor's found a free man named Geer. Building a mill and needs a man to help."

In Jute's mind, the job already sure, the unknown pay no longer questioned, the man, a dim figure promising much.

"When we meet we'll talk of wages and a place for you."

"I could stay here," Susu began timidly, the thought of moving another upheaval in her mind.

"You'll go where I go," said Jute, leaving much still unsettled. Turning, he went to bed.

\* \* \*

Jute'd said after Christmas!

It arrived with snow, quiet all around.

Back home Susu knew the day. Field men didn't work none. More time allowed for church. The recollected singing, stomping, joy of it pealed Susu's heart. Memories of swaying bodies, arm on arm — Momma, Poppa, Jute, joined! Hogs juicing on the spits.

Clara Martin'd placed an orange on Susu's tray. Brushed back her new cropped hair. "God go with you child," she said.

Susu smelled duck cooking. Her sums and book neglected. Even the knitting she was trying to finish lay forgotten.

Moving on — a hollow sound — another unknown! She missed the door pushed open. Jute standing there noted her blank face.

"Tomorrow, tomorrow I go to see about the job!"

Used only to her cowed acceptance from the first, he was unready for flying fur. She turned the fury of trapped animal eyes on him, but the expected accompanying word torrent never came.

"Here," he said. Putting something within reach on the chest of drawers.

Without touching, Susu devoured the doll, made like the one carried so long, skirt'n all, painted face, corn cob body. She searched for his face, but Jute'd turned staring out the window at the carriage house below.

"An' 'fix yerself up some." The other gift, a thick brush. Frayed at one side, a short stocky hickory branch, cut to fit her hand.

She'd thought he never noticed when Clara Martin chopped off any extra length of hair, her scissors reached, never cared. A choked back sob filled Susu's throat.

"Reach about," she said pointing under the bed.

He pulled out the crutches wondering.

Practiced now, Susu turned deftly on her good leg. Clearing the door and Jute, she swung steadily down the hall. He watched, beginning to realize what practice went into her effort.

"Got a stick whittled, been saving till you could get about," he said gruffly before he left.

Susu returned to her high bed. He'd not been going to go on without her! She fingered the new doll, feeling better about pushing on.

Jute hitched the bay early Wednesday before he was asked. The horse, used to him, puffed out white billows in the frosted air. Goes was farther North than Jute'd gone before. He drove, Dr. Sammison settling in beside him, talking little, his hands beneath the muffling robe he'd tucked over his knees. Jute shuffled his feet in the doctor's old shoes worn since the ground was hard. Wishing to ask a lot, settled for crumbs of conversation the doctor spilled between long spells of thought.

"Wilson Geer has youngsters. Susu can help with tending those now she can move about some, using that big stick you've whittled, and much can be done sitting down."

Jute listened, wondering if that man Geer still needed to be sold on the idea. They crossed a covered bridge and doubled back down a long lane of trees beside the river. This'll be the place, he thought. The importance of that unknown man curled his spine. Would he be safe here? Was he tucked far enough away from the evil outside world? Never!

The house was small but well made. A window on each side of the door, a cabin shed and barn out back, stained brown like the house, gave the place a neat and homey air. They drove around behind. The buggy was tied before a large man, crossing to a stile in the lower pasture near the river, cleared it wih two steps. His body was massive, his face, the color of wet sand, could've been graven out of rock. He looked at Jute as some men skim a horse, just a flickered glance up and down and up again, then spoke to the doctor.

"Thought he'd be bigger, someway more growed. Hefty work, setting up a mill. The stones alone'll weigh a heap."

Jute forgot his panic and spoke out. He'd not come this far to be stopped by a man's notions of what he could or couldn't do.

"I've lifted bales of tobacco from light to light, 'fore I was growed," he said. "Then traveled over mountains folks said couldn't be crossed, sometimes toting my sister and our things. Nothing stopped me an' wouldn've but her leg got broke and we's bogged down here till it's mended."

Geer's eyes flickered over Jute, his interest lit at the hot tone in Jute's voice.

"Guess you'll do, but I can't pay you none," he said.

The words hit Jute a blow he'd not expected. A job for pay'd been the price he'd set for stopping short of freedom. He stood, not knowing how to refuse to do the job he'd hankered for this long.

The doctor stepped up.

"Jute's never had wages," he said, his quiet voice as certain as the blood running in Jute's temples. The mill will bring you hard cash come spring. I gave my word there'd be some pay for this work, as well as lodging for him and his sister here."

"Them with no freedom papers and a fine or more for me if they be caught?" countered Geer. "God's toadstool, you drive a mean bargin, doctor."

"And who's got the better right till Goes gets a doctor closer'n Xenia?"

The glance between the men was like a silken cord so strong Jute felt he could reach out and pull it, feel its promise.

Neither man backed down till Geer said, "Five dollars a month for him an' food for both, provided he's a good worker an' stays till the mill's done. I don't want someone who'll drift off with the first freedom train. He kin stay on for double, once the mill's fetching profit."

The doctor reached out a soft hand, soon hidden in Geer's giant grasp. Geer shook Jute's hand, too. The strength of it caught him unready to clasp back with what he had. Geer turned beckoning both men toward the house

"You've not seen Miz Geer since the babe came early."

A young woman was by the door. Round and soft, she looked as if she'd always been a mother. Two children, little tots, hung to her skirts, peeping out with sticky jam covered mouths. A suckling infant, held in place by a sling shawl, left her hands free for tasks. She answered the doctor's questions about the baby in a pleasant quiet voice, her answers smooth and short.

Susu will like it here, thought Jute, and with the thought he looked about the place for the first time. Most of the furnishings homemade, sturdy. The solid table, flanked by benches, had dents where children's spoons had banged the wood. Even board floor met the stone hearth, brushed, clean.

The doctor looked the youngsters over before he left.

"No one ailing, thank God," Geer's wife breathed as they prepared to go. The doctor shook his head when she asked him to stay and share a meal. "We'll be home in time for dinner," he said.

It was the following Saturday before Jute returned to Geer's, this time with Susu wedged into the buggy, her shawl about her head and shoulders, and the big stick she now used tucked at her side. Mr. Martin drove them to Goes, his stiff back straight, not touching the driver's seat.

Susu looked around at bare branches and countryside she hadn't seen since she peeked out between the slats of the cattle car with Leah. Where were Leah and her mother now, and all the others? She felt the hollow answer. She'd never know.

## CHAPTER FIFTEEN

## The Mill

It was late afternoon before they reached the mill. Jute lifted Susu out of the buggy. She hobbled eagerly to the cabin door, the sharp point of her stick skidding on the melting ice of a winter thaw. The walk leading to the little house all slidey. Only when checkered light from the small side window crossed her path did she remember that these were strangers. Jute'd described the youngsters she'd be caring for, Mr. Geer, and the work to be done at the mill, so often, seemed as if she'd met them herself last Wednesday with Dr. Sammison.

"A job with pay," he'd said. "At last I got me a real job—for a while", he'd add more darkly. "For a while."

He'd come to her room nights with a glint she hadn't seen since he was spiking freedom talk with the men back home. Talking to her for a change 'bout plans ahead.

Susu turned round. Why was Jute taking so long with their things and the buggy? Maybe the Geers didn't know about her broken leg, how hard it was to get about. Maybe they wouldn't want her, nor Jute neither, if'n they knew.

Before Susu worked herself into a true fright, the door opened. The Geers stood framed in their own firelight. Two little ones about two years old, the mister, missus, and a baby, just as Jute'd said, smiling welcome at her as if part of their family'd come home. Susu knew she'd like it here. She'd work hard for Miz Geer an' the babies. Come spring Dr. Sammison'd said she wouldn't need her stick t' walk down by the river no more.

Belonging was more important to Susu than freedom. She could belong with these people. Miz Geer's skin, lighter than her own, was the rich brown cocoa color of Momma's. Her dark eyes wide, smiling like Momma's eyes used to when she smiled at Susu busy with her dolls and little chips of dishes.

She reached out an arm to steady Susu over the rough stone step leading to the front door, while Mr. Geer went out to show Jute round back to the shed where he'd sleep.

"You kin put a chimney in during your free hours," Susu heard him say as the men rounded the corner of the house.

The door shut. Susu felt shyness slip back around her. The little ones, too, edged away from her, behind their mother once more.

The baby wailed.

"Hush", said Miz Geer. "What's your name, child?"

\* \* \*

Susu felt at ease from that first day. She slept in a broad low trundle bed near the big one, Seth and Dan tucked on either side. She went to bed when they did after the last dishes were wiped, stacked for the morning meal, next to the pot of oats set out for breakfast. She grew used to feeling their warm bodies burrowing on either side, the soft lapping sound as they suckled fingers in the dark. They'd giggle and poke her when they woke. Curling an arm under each frizzled head, Susu pretended to clunk them together in a morning ritual begun the first day. Laughing, all three'd tumble out of bed to dress in the cold dark morning.

Susu hopped about without her stick, shivering, as she helped the twins into their drawers, woolen socks and shoes. The long warm gowns they kept on night and day, with a camphor bag hung around their necks to keep away the croup. Susu still slept in the fine tucked gown that'd belonged to Millie Sammison and changed into a dress of hers that Clara Martin'd cut down to size, with the home spun top Mrs. Bartlett'd taught her to knit. She brushed her short hair back and pinned it like Clara'd showed her how. She had a box from Dr. Jim for her things. The book of flowers, her new doll, brush, her copybook and pencils, kept away from sticky fingers on a high shelf. Her own collection, started fresh.

All day she played with the little boys and helped Miz Geer when she could. The baby stayed at its mother's side, wrapped in his sling, suckled, or in his cradle near the fire. Dan was the quiet twin, his round face always smiling. Seth, the bigger one, was hard to catch. He'd run around the table, and turning suddenly, duck under it to escape Susu's halting limp, if it was time for a wash or dose of camomile. She'd invent games to bring him round when he got out of sorts.

They never went out in the cold winter air. Miz Geer was that afraid of their catching some winter complaint. They liked to roll a spool, hearing it click on the wide floor boards. They made pebble pictures using the smooth round stones Susu brought in from the path. Nights, Jute carved them acorn rings to slip on and off their pudgy fingers and hickory rattles from dried burrs he picked up near the barn. Sometimes Susu read to them from her flower book.

"That's real pretty," Miz Geer'd say, as if to make up for the squirming boys who left as soon as the picture page was turned.

Susu tried to be a help, to be a grown girl and not another child around the house. Miz Geer was always busy.

"I helped old Sarah with the wash at home," Susu said one day when shooed off again with the twins to play. "I could do it alone here. There's so much less."

"Later, child, when your leg's full healed and it's warm enough for the boys to run outside," said Miz Geer. "There's time enough. I used to do it all, and with the twins hanging on my skirts. You do fine keeping them busy. Don't fret so child."

There were things Susu could do sitting down. She pared apples, fixed vegetables, wound skeins of wool, and kneaded dough. She felt as if this'd always been her home. One day followed the next in an easy round of living. She lost track of how long they'd been at the mill.

* * *

From the first day there, Jute'd felt more a man. He'd little enough to stow away in the small shed room, but it was his place all the same. Not attached to any other. He planned to start a chimney, like Geer said, with stones dug from the creek bed, held steady with caked mud till it dried there solid. He'd find time 'tween mill work and feeding animals. When that was done, he'd cut an opening in the wall and build a hearth.

Much work'd already been done on the mill by the day when Jute arrived. The mill run dug and lined with timber, dam begun, huge flat stones swelled the creek that flowed high even in winter till it reached the tangled roots a few feet from its banks. The tall mill structure towered over the water, timbered in with beams so broad Jute didn't see how men could've set them into place. Even a double brace of men Geer's size would've been hard put to raise them there.

"It's almost finished," Jute said, when he first looked up toward the hoist three stories from the ground.

Disappointed, he'd come to finish the job, if he decided to stay.

"Not by a sparrow's eye," said Geer. "I hired some men to get it under roof, but now all the inside fixin's still to be done 'fore winter's past. An' there's a water wheel to fashion, iron work, belts to be hung for totin' corn up to the lift, mill stones t' be brought an' set in for grindin'. We'll be jim-lucky t' have all that done by spring. Being January next week."

Even while he talked, Geer's hands were busy, planing down the outside door. Swollen with the weather, it wouldn't latch. Jute picked up the shavings, ramming them into a bin where others'd been saved for starting cook fires. He hankered for a bigger job to prove his strength against this giant.

He looked at Geer. If Dr. Sammison'd been true, Geer was a man like him, born slave, but set free in manhood. Couldn't happen to him.

"How'd you learn t' figger all this?" Jute waved an arm taking in the mill work already done.

"Readin' comes first," said Geer. "Plans is all set down here." He tapped a well-thumbed book set on a table just inside the door, a stool in front of it, an oil lamp for reading nights. "Sent for it more'n a year back."

"You'll learn soon enough once you're settled an' really start to work. Pay day's last o' the month, an' Sunday's t' yerself, save feeding of the animals about the place."

Jute nodded and walked back to the shed. He'd've whistled, but thought it might sound lightheaded, so he turned and walked a pace before looking back at the unfinished mill standing square over the river. A lot to do yet, Geer'd said. He could keep up with any job set forward, and show them the man he had become!

The morning after breakfast with the family, Jute helped to lay the heavy flooring on the second story of the mill. Broad boards cut at the saw mill downriver were stacked high outside the door. It took both men to angle them into place and pound long nails in to the steady wood below. Behind them the floor stretched even. In front, a skeleton of beams waited to be covered. Jute pushed hard, his wiry frame keeping stride with Geer's bulky one. Half a floor was done when the winter sun washed white through bare branches tapping the mill roof at noon. Geer stood up and shoved back the kerchief tied round his brow.

"Let's eat," he said, shimmying down the narrow ladder. They set off for the house.

As the days marched toward that first pay day the mill took shape under the steady beat of work and will. If I stay, still rattled Jute's head, bumping into, when I leave. But he thought on learning too. He'd toted numbers on tobacco bales back home, some letters even. Could he search out meaning from printed picture pages? Shape a water wheel? Should he stay till he'd seen it done? He lay in bed nights, tired, sore, his race to keep up with Geer as wearying as the trek across the mountains. He tried to stay awake picturing what lay ahead, but never got beyond thinking of the finished mill, working, grinding, wagons coming down Jacoby Road with corn, leaving with sacks of meal piled higher than the gate.

Never got to mulling over Canada, finding a train, leaving, though his plan still hovered there unformed. Some other time, he'd think, when wages was put by.

Pay day was cold and clear, without snow, January 31. Jute remembered when he went to bed wondering if Wilson Geer'd let him have the rig to get to town. Didn't have long to wait that morning. Geer brought the subject up himself.

"We need another keg of nails," he said, "and a telegraph sent to check the order for mill stones. Those New York men never did answer the letter I sent last summer. Maybe you and Susu'd like to go. I'll stay home with Miz Geer and the babes."

Jute'd dreamed on it. A trip to town. But now possible he saw the mishaps that could occur. Dr. Sammison'd always told him to lay low no matter how many glory tales he heard. When he did go out it was always with the doctor, counting on his silver tongue and reputation to explain why Jute was there.

To go alone now? They had too much to lose.

Don't think so, was on his lips to say, but Geer, noting his passing thoughts, stared him down.

"Too feared?" he said flaunting the dare. "Can't hide forever. Life's for living."

Spitting mad, Jute said. "You aint paid me yet. When do we leave?"

"After breakfast and chores," said Geer.

He counted out the five dollars, each one clinking into Jute's palm with a ring he'd not forget.

Later that morning when Susu was feeding chickens out back, Jute came near and whispered in her ear.

"Know what day this is?"

A cold fear clutched her heart. Feeling so much at home she'd lost track of the days. Forgot to be frightened as at the doctors. Was it the day to be moving on?

Jute didn't seem mad no more, but he'd never give up Canada. She didn't know how far it was from here. Didn't want to be stirring no more, no matter what. Her face must have shown the panic she felt.

Jute laughed out loud and shook her arm.

"What ails you, goose girl? It's pay day! Whole month's over!"

He slapped his leg and laughed again.

"You and me is going on a buying spree. Geer needs supplies. Said we could take the wagon into town."

Susu and Jute sat up on the seat behind the slow plodding horse Geer used for all heavy hauling on the place. House windows sparked as they approached town. Sometimes a man out front or children too small for school looked up as they passed. Jute stared back. Hiding fear. He thought, gots a job rightful, an' folks to speak up why I'se here.

Still smarting from Geer's challenge, Jute felt more a man. As if its purpose was to keep him alert. Defying it met his inner need. He glanced over his shoulder often, protecting his shanks as well as points ahead. A busy town on market day. Jute saw other blacks as well as whites doing business.

Susu clutched the message written out for him to send, as if she thought it'd take wings and fly east by itself before Jute could send it from the station.

They did Geer's job first. Selecting nails, Jute gave the keg a shake and looked through several handsful carefully, checking for rust and bent ends. Susu at the other side of the store savored peppermint balls and licorice whips with her eyes.

Buying their own things took time.

Jute chose a stout pair of winter boots, first he'd had new for himself, with laces tied together, and shining silver eyelets.

"Put them on and wear them home," said Susu, smoothing their rounded toes, remembering when her shoes were new.

"Time enough for that." Jute fingered the coins remaining and eyed a pair of red and green braces to replace his frayed hemp belt.

"How much?" he asked the storekeeper.

Jute's boots and braces, a real comb for Susu, and a twist of peppermints and licorice left him fifty cents. Walking down to the depot where they tied the horse, Jute noticed Susu's limp was on the mend. A slight jogging step was all that was left to remind him of the accident and their delayed plans. No reason we can't go on now.

He left her in the wagon and went inside to send the message to Boston. Mill stones sent from France'd stop on the East Coast first. They weren't due till spring, but Geer was itching to hear some sure word of how far along his shipment'd come. Business done, Jute lingered at the counter for a bit, looking at chalked numbers on the slate behind the ticket agent. They made no sense.

"Anything else?" the man asked, noticing Jute still peering through the bars.

"Two tickets for Canada? How much'd they be?" he asked surprising himself more than the agent.

"Depends on where — Ottawa, Montreal, Quebec?"

"Closest," answered Jute.

"Seven-fifty apiece, change at Detroit," answered the man.

Jute turned, starting out of the depot. He saw a man emerging, near Susu and the wagon. Long and spare, he had a nervous way of ticking his head over one shoulder leaving an expanse of red seamed neck on the other side, sticking out of his collar like a chicken about to get the ax. He brushed his hand across his sandy mustache setting his broad rimmed hat upon his head more than once.

Always twitching, thought Jute. Bad sign. What's he after? Should scam, but Geer's rig, Susu... He didn't want to meet this man.

"New to Xenia?" drawled the stranger, southern-like, to Jute still standing on the depot step.

Lies raced through Jute's mind.

"Yes," he said, deciding to stay with the truth, "work for Wilson Geer, down Jacoby Creek."

"Recognized the horse. I'm blacksmith hereabouts." The man grasped the bridle with a proprietorial hand. "You'll be needin' papers go or stay even north t' be legal y' know," he said. "We'll talk on it when you got the coin."

Untying the wagon he handed the reins to Jute, slapped the horse's rump sharply, and turned toward the center of town, snaking his way without a backward glance.

Coin! He'd not pay this man to keep him free.

Jute said nothing on the trip home, not answering Susu's chatter, even with a nod.

Fifteen dollars! He'd have about that much when the mill was done — not before — but now he couldn't stay. Had to be pushing on — tomorrow! This man spelled danger; the odor was all around him. As if he knew only fifty cents remained! His plan upset, had to be changed somehow.

## CHAPTER SIXTEEN

### The Water Wheel

Escape plans turned in Jute's head faster'n wagon wheels. Susu wasn't up to foot travel an' he didn't have papers, or money yet for trains. . . .

Perhaps Geer'd help, but would it set well t'leave before his promise?

The family was settling in when they got back. Morning would have to be soon enough. He ranged his shed room unable to sleep. He'd felt safe working here. Fears of chasing-men dimmed. Gone soft, thought Jute, bitter, but still can shove on—me'n Susu both.

Geer recognized the description Jute gave of the man he'd seen.

That'll be Springer, the blacksmith, I've dealt with him before. H'aint heard he doles us dark folks harm. Maybe thought you's out to take my wagon. Stay boy, I'll mosey round—warn you if something's up—I hear most things.

Jute turned to lash out. To say he'd go when he pleased, but had no better plan in mind. "We'll stay fer now."

Warning his promise might be broke, made him feel better.

They'd both keep out an eye. No soft perch from here on.

All February Geer and Jute fashioned the wheel from plans in the book on how to build a mill. The soaked lumber bent full circle at last, three boards thick, its buckets standing firm on every spoke.

"Neighbors'll come to help," Geer'd said when Jute asked about how they would set the monstrous wheel in place. "We need all the workers we can get to set it in place."

It had to turn under the mill, bolted into a housing of its own.

Jute began to realize how many people they were expecting when Miz Geer and Susu started baking two days before, setting out food in the keeper.

"We'll feed 'em all, and their families, those as come," said Geer that morning, looking out for signs of late winter snow.

Although the ground was frozen hard, skies were clear, when wagons and rigs began to fill the yard.

The Browns and Kings came first. The nearest neighbors, they were well known by Jute. They'd come to borrow things or pass the time most every week. Freemen like Geer, they'd bought in the valley early as Geer'd done when land, far from any sizable town, was cheap. Two white men followed.

"Hollack, Springer." Geer acknowledged their greetings and tied their wagons as he had the others.

Suspicion darkened Jute's day with a scowl. Why would these men step out to help?

Springer, the very one'd kept him losing sleep. Why here? Why now? Harm meant fer sure! The work was hard and no one compensated beyond knowing there'd be a mill handy come fall. He edged away from the newcomers. They weren't Quakers—like ones'd helped him starting out. Didn't have their black clothes or soft spoken ways. One a farmer, hands and face weathered by hard times, same's Geer's, one blacksmith. Coulter, a black man Jute'd seen before, was last to arrive. His wife and children bundled into the house, he joined the others at the barn.

"Jute here's my hand," said Geer noticing the newcomers glancing over in Jute's direction, open curiosity on their faces. "He's come lately. Brought by Dr. Sammison."

Jute didn't like the way they kept looking at him as if the questions in their minds couldn't be spoken out clear. How'd he know they wouldn't turn a fast dollar—soon's they left, reporting him and Geer for hiring free.

Hollack was stolid, slow, but packed a mighty heft when they started working. Seemed Springer's friend. Both to be distrusted.

The men braced the wheel against their shoulders and rolled it to the nearest point of the housing they could reach, then pushed and shoved and hoisted it in place. Bigger than any three men together, the wheel completed, was an awesome sight, bulky, thick.

"Hell boiling over," cursed Coulter as a sliver from the wheel drew blood under his thumbnail.

Jute, picked because of his slight frame and climbing skill, lowered himself into the housing, turning the big bolts in place as the puffing men below strained to hold it there, level. The groaning wheel hitched slightly and shivered in its casing. Jute looked down once, black water below dizzying him with its rushing sound. He almost lost balance, but clutching the wrench firmly in his hand, he twisted each bolt as tight as it'd go into the axle. He forgot his precarious position, and that the wheel could slip, crushing him beneath its shattering weight.

Jute worked on till the last pin was fastened. Finally, letting out his breath with a whistle, he climbed out to stand near Coulter, brow glistening and proud.

Geer thumped the wheel a mighty blow to see if it would shift or shimmy. Then, pulling up the gate to the sluiceway, he let more water in. Gushing, bubbling, it soon filled the spillway.

The big wheel turned slowly at first, but as the buckets filled it gained speed, beating a steady rhythm, muffled, hollow, in the cellar of the mill. A good sound, one Jute got used to quick, as if he'd always heard it there. It became a part of him, turning, turning, like a new heartbeat he couldn't live without.

"Couldn't have trundled it without your help," Geer told the men.

"Mine'll be the first corn ground, and the best," bragged Brown, slapping Geer on the shoulder.

"Have to put in a regular railroad run to the bank in Xenia, once the news gets around you're open for business," said Hollack.

"Not so fast. Mill stones haven't come."

"Heard anything?"

"I expect they're ice-bound in the East. Jute sent a telegraph last month, but no word yet. They cost a pile and weigh a heap each. We'll have to build a special wagon to drag them from the train," said Geer.

At the sound of his name Jute drew back a bit, standing within the shadow of the housing post. He'd forgot trying to avoid attention. Uneasy about men he didn't know. Springer seemed too interested—gave him a bad feeling he'd learned to trust, about men and their intentions. He hung back to speak to Jute as the others, full of talk of crops and threatened war, drifted toward the house and food.

"Where you from, 'fore Sammison's, I mean?" he asked, so direct and clear Jute couldn't avoid answering, fearing it could be checked.

"Down t' Maryland," he answered.

"How come you working here?"

"My sister's leg got broke on the way north. We stayed a bit to let it heal."

God blast his nosey ways. Now the whole story split so open he'd have to be shoving fast no matter what Geer said. And Susu thriving here under Miz Geer's care. Her heart wasn't set to run again yet.

Springer moved along toward the house, adding nothing to his questions to help Jute know what he was thinking. Jute, silent too, thought of the money put by, not enough for tickets yet — not quite.

Inside the house the big table was pushed in the middle of the room. Every bench and chair used, some still standing. The women'd put out food and crockery for all. Coulter's merry wife, her brown face smiling, helped with dishes she'd brought, adding a party air. Hungry men slumped, worn out from shifting the heavy wheel. Miz Geer handed Jute a plate, ham and beans with corn bread and apple butter. A mug of cider in his other hand, Jute found an empty place on a bench. Sitting down, he settled his mug between his feet. He'd keep an eye on them all from here he thought. Might not seem natural for him to scamp before the meal.

Susu helped the women. She'd learned to work and keep the little ones out from under foot. One twin on Geer's knee was sucking his thumb and listening to the men, while the other trailed along after Susu for the raisins and bits of buttered cornbread she'd hand him from time to time.

"Can't pick up a newspaper without it screaming of another state threatening to secede," said Hollack. "Let them go, and good riddance, I'd say. We can do without the whole South and still have a country good as any."

"We can do without them and their crops," answered Geer," but it'll give that new President a devil of a time if he tries to hold on to property down South, like he promised.

Jute noticed that Springer was silent as he. Chewing his food, moving his head in that queer way he had. It wasn't long before the crowd thinned, getting on home to do their own chores.

Springer and Hollack left together. Coulter was last. His wife, visiting on with Miz Geer, had no time for the children. She sent them spinning off outside to play, bidding them stay on the step near Susu, as she tied up bundles of tin mugs and a stack of extra plates she'd brought from home. Susu gathered the little ones around her. Holding two on a crowded lap she sat on the step playing patty cake, clapping their hands together with a great squeeze at the end. She gave Coulter's three a turn and was starting over with the littlest when it was time for them to leave.

Things soon seemed back to normal. Geer and Jute, finishing up in the barn, stopped to watch the wheel on their way home from tending the animals. They stood silent, listening for a while to the unfamiliar flow of water under the mill house where none'd been before.

"It's going to be good to see those stones set in and grinding corn, all that yellow meal filling sacks from those chutes up there."

The want to see it too, finished and working, drove Jute to speak before he thought things out.

"I'm leaving," he said.

"I know," said Geer. "In good time you'll want a place of your own."

"No, now," said Jute, urgently, his voice even softer than before, realizing for the first time it would hurt to see the end of a place, hurt him as well as Susu.

"But why? You said you'd see me through the winter, till the mill was done and working."

"That man, Springer," Jute began. "I don't tote the way he looks at me, suspicious like. Like he aimed to get us both in trouble. Like he was scheming something. All that way on the mountain alone, and down at the river when I spotted dock workers about to turn us in. I knows people. I sniff 'em out like guide dogs. I almost lost it here, having a safe place to sleep every night, but I feel it now, hard, and I'm scared for us all. He warned me before. He won't wait forever."

"I don't know Springer, but I know Hollack some," said Geer. He wasn't scoffing at Jute, not disagreeing neither.

"Tell you what." He looked at the darkening skies. "I'll ride over and sound Hollack out a bit. Tell Miz Geer I'll be there, but don't alarm her none, nor Susu neither."

Jute agreed, and saying as little as he could, he let Miz Geer know Geer'd be back 'fore long.

In the shed Jute gathered together things he'd bought in town, his hidden cache of money, a very little pile.

Couldn't worry on Susu. He glanced at his chimney, not finished enough to lay a fire. All that blamed talk of secession, war! And "I'm not free yet," he muttered to himself. "One man with an ornery face can make me run, even here, where I've come to feel easy. I'll never stay put till I'm somewhere legal. Till no man has lief to lay a hand on me, nor Susu neither."

Discouragement soaked his every bone, weary from the heavy work beneath the wheel. He lay down on his bunk to wait for Geer's return. In nightmare dreams he looked over his shoulder at every step for Springer's overtaking stride.

## CHAPTER SEVENTEEN

## Mill Stones

Jute heard Geer come into the yard sometime after dark. Awakened, he lay on the bunk waiting for a knock. Five minutes passed. Geer wasn't coming.

"Might've at least told me what Hollack said, " he grumbled.

Getting up, he paced the cramped shed, outlines of furnishings just visible in the dark. After a bit he gave up, lying down again on the narrow bed. Couldn't have been anything too bad. Geer would've warned us to get out tonight. He tried to breathe a bit easier. Might see this job finished yet, stay till spring when Susu's leg was really healed, the mill working.

But nothing set him back to the easy feeling he'd had. Springer's spying talk at the depot, his sly looks here. Got to get, he planned silently. Can't call no place home yet.

Nothing was said over breakfast, the air of the little house heavy with unanswered questions. Meeting down at the mill, Geer spoke first.

"Hollack says Springer's just interested in where you come from. Claims he'd a hand in bringing folks North at the last place he lived over at Marietta. He'd a regular run there, organized by some abolitionist preacher, who paid him by the wagon load each night he slipped through to the next county."

"Admits he's a man interested in turning his hand to coin whereever he finds it. Round about it's making papers for folks who wants to travel above board." Geer wiped damp palms through his hair, forehead to nape and back again, "Could be he'd turn you in if you didn't buy, to keep his name clean with the law. Don't know, I'll keep sharp eyes."

Wasn't good enough to settle Jute.

The puzzle worked on him. If'n he paid Springer he'd have no travelin' cash, he'd have to work longer for train fare, but if'n he didn't.... All day he pounded foundation spikes needlessly. Muscles keeping pace with his spinning brain, pondering the riddle. Sweat ran off his brow, splashing his cheek, drenching his shirt from armpits blackened with its soak.

He twisted the slicked handle of the huge mallet he'd been using, as if wringing the neck of this new enemy causing him so much grief. He spat out his decision to Geer.

"I'll buy the varmit's sham, when I can, come spring. Till then he'd better keep clear of me. Let Hollack know. I'm shoving on May 1st with or without his pulp."

Knotted swollen hands on the thick smooth wood betrayed the grating threat in Jute's voice. So riled, no one could've told bossman from worker. Standing, fists clenched, hissing orders, Jute wasn't no man to refute.

All March kept them working on the pulleys that would lower sacks of grain to the main floor. Jute nailed them into place while Geer knotted heavy rope and gave the wheel trial spins to see if the knot would catch or the line freeze.

Building the big cart needed to drag the heavy buhrstones home from the Xenia station was the largest job.

April arrived with planting chores to keep their minds off the shipment still not arrived from the East.

After a day in the fields Jute and Geer would slip into the mill separately, each checking the equipment standing ready for the big stones to be set in place. Jute knew the mill book almost as well as Geer by now. He'd figure pages as they worked, step by step, to the end. Geer explained words Jute didn't understand. They measured each working part over'n over to be sure it matched the plans. Since March they'd had time to review some of the work Geer'd done early on. Jute dreamed of one day building a mill of his own in Canada.

Susu'd changed too, skipping outside with the little ones trailing after her, almost as if she'd never had to lean on a cane dragging a foot behind her. The remaining limp hardly showed and didn't slow her down none. Jute's pile of cash grew with each payday. Hoarding now, he almost had the price of tickets to Ottawa if'n he didn't buy passes from Springer. Hadn't begun to figure on how to slip clear of the man, but he would.

It would cause them both a pang to leave, but freedom 'd been the price he'd set. Stopping short wasn't Jute's plan. Couldn't be.

Susu and the twins strayed down to the creek one budding day mid-April and missed seeing the man ride up on horseback shouting Geer's name.

"He's off to the south pasture," said Jute.

"A shipment from Boston's come. Station master says I should tell him myself. Said it was that important."

"I'll see Mr. Geer gets your message, Sir." said Miz Geer. Leaving the baby in the basket near the washline, she stood at the fence talking to the man. Her quiet air quelled his hesitation. Not looking further, he turned and rode back to town.

"I'll go down t' tell him." Jute's excitement rose at thoughts of stones set in place, the mill working!

He started at a run across an unplowed field to where Geer, steadying a fencepost with an extra twist of wire, bent, eyes on his work. Glancing up, he knew immediately why Jute was hurrying so. Listening as Jute repeated the message, twice, he looked up. Early afternoon sun was still high in the mottled April sky.

"Too late to go today. It'll take four trips starting off early. Two tomorrow and two the next day."

The plan'd long been laid for bringing the stones home. Everyone would go. Miz Geer, Susu and the young ones remaining in town between trips to visit and shop. Miz Geer's Aunt Mara lived in Xenia.

Geer, usually so steady, looked as if he might skip one minute and break into nervous sweats the next. He was full of worries. Every penny he could scrape had gone into the purchase and shipping of these stones.

"You don't think one could've cracked?" he fretted as they were waiting for Miz Geer and Susu to ready the children early the next day.

"Crate'n all, they should ride easy in this cart." He tested again the sides and wheels of the sturdy wagon built specially for heavy loads of corn after the stones were safely installed. The two plodding horses, already hitched, stared ahead unmoving as if studying the trampled ground. The second one, a recent addition, bought with this trip in mind, matched the first. "A pair any man could be proud of," Geer'd remarked.

Miz Geer, buttoning the small boys into their first trousers, gave each a final pat. Town clothes, clean and new. Their rosy brown cheeks glowed with excitement at the thought of two days outing and a long ride in the new cart filled with straw to cushion the precious load. "We're ready, Mr. Geer," she said.

A gala day for Susu from the start. She handed the baby, wrapped in a fringed shawl against uncertain weather, up to its mother, now waiting patiently on the high board seat. Geer helped settle his boys. Nesting in barn-dried straw, they snuggled beside Susu. She propped her healed leg on the basket holding food and glanced at Jute, sitting behind facing the rear. Back straight, he waited for Geer to untie the reins, impatient to get moving at last.

Jute didn't talk much about plans now, but she knew about the money tied in a sock beneath a stone in the newly laid hearth. This'd not be the last place they'd be stopping. Wasn't Canada, but it surely was the best. She couldn't think on roaming.

Danny and Seth began to bounce at her side like to fly out the cart before it started. They were dear to her as anyone she'd known back home, save Momma. Miz Geer didn't take Momma's place none, but growed like she was, was more like having a sister, a heap older with children of her own.

The spring day turned warm and sunny. April shoots showed green on bushes and trees along the carriage road. Everything smelled new. Mixed with the sound of scrabbling rocks under their wooden wheels, she could hear the chorus of birds and cheepers returning north. The baby soon lulled to sleep by the jogging motion of the cart.

Geer threw back his head and sang a song Jute remembered from the tobacco fields: "The big wheel turns by faith, And the little one turns by the hand of God. Wheel within a wheel, Way in the middle of the air."

Jute couldn't join the festive mood of the occasion. Each turn brought him closer to leaving. He now had ten dollars in the secret place he stored his money. Next pay-day, the mill completed, would make it fifteen—enough for railfare to Canada! The fright he felt about Springer kept his determination hot. By heaven, I'll never again get so I forget danger could still come in the form of any weasel as chooses to turn us in, he vowed, not forgetting the sudden stab of terror.

He remembered men trailed from farther than he'd come, dragged back beaten, chained. He looked at Susu riding so happy, flanked by the babies that loved her as though her kin. He wouldn't tell her yet. Wouldn't spoil a minute of her holiday. Let everything get set, tickets bought. Then, goodbyes said quick, as before times — only harder.

* * *

They reached Xenia before noon, turning toward the brick depot away from the market square. A crowd around the place made Wilson Geer smile.

"They've come to view my shipment," he said. "Not every day one gets to see buhrstones all the way from France."

Boys were waving flags, small children with hoops and dogs all chased each other on the cluttered yard of the big brick depot close to town. People in clusters stood about as if it was Sunday, and they had no place to go, church being over. A train halted in progress, faces pressed against the windows, everyone talking together as if they knew each other.

Some of those passengers must be strangers to the Xenia crowd, thought Jute, taking in the jumbled scene with a puzzled air.

Susu'd never seen so many people. It added to her pleasure at the day away from home and chores.

The underlying current of excitement surpassed Geer's own. His horses, stopped by the press of bodies in the street, were blocked from further passage toward the train. His mood changed to impatience, then anger, at this delay. He muttered curses under his breath at the people in his way, cluttering up the street, obviously not here because of him.

"Thunderation! Can't a man do business with this railroad, and you have your picnic or holiday somewhere less busy? I've two loads to fetch by nightfall," he roared.

No one paying him no mind, thought Jute. Geer's temper went unnoticed by the crowd.

"Jute, hop down and see what's keeping us from the freight yard."

Jute made his way through the buzzing crowd, bent on his mission. He hammered on the freight office door, surprised to see it closed this time of day. He rapped again sharply on the lettered glass door proclaiming the hours: Weekdays Open 8 to 6

Through the glass Jute could see the huge stones in their sturdy crates, each one broader than a man could span, filling the office with their bulk. Smooth gray stone between the slats, carved, ready to complete the mill. He raised his fist to pound again.

A touch on his shoulder made him swing around, suspicious at any man's hand laid on him. "Won't be no business done this day," said a man nearby.

"Got to get Mr. Geer's buhrstones, they're locked up in there," Jute yelled above the din. "He aims to have them in his cart right quick."

"Ain't you heard?" The man looked at Jute like he was from another world. "This ain't no regular day of business. Fort Sumter down in South Carolina's been fired on by Southerners, and war's begun."

The words buzzed round Jute's head like flies in August. Men went on, talking around him making little sense.

"All those seceding states banding together to fight us, to fight every durn state that doesn't hold with slavery, the whole North!"

"Yes, and they'll get their tails bit off before summer and come running home to lick their wounds," chimed a stranger, eager to inform anyone who hadn't yet heard the news.

Jute looked up and saw Geer's head pushing behind him in the crowd. Too impatient to wait for Jute's return, he'd followed him into the throng. By his slack jaw and changing expression, Jute knew he too was hearing talk about the war. His face filled with emotion, he doubled his efforts to get to Jute.

War! Jute tried to bring back what Dr. Sammison had said last fall when they were riding in the buggy.

"If it comes to war, you'll be as free hereabouts as anywhere in Canada. The promised land then'll be what you make it, Son."

Struggling to take it all in, a shout born in his toes almost burst his chest. "We're free, Susu! We're free!" he bellowed over the heads of the crowds, pushing toward the wagon to tell her. "We made it. We can stay."

Geer reached him first, his strong arm braced Jute and stayed there in a crushing hug. Jute searched his face and saw he knew it too, saw it was really true. Geer's heavy hand gripped Jute's work shirt and suspenders as he steered him to the others.

Jute could see Susu, leaning forward, taking in the scattered mob. Her sharp little face was smiling, eager, her hair pulled back the way she'd worn it lately, making her look older than ten. Now he'd never have to tell her they must leave.

She'll be free, too, to learn, grow up how she likes, to marry and have babies that wouldn't never be taken away.

"You've won your gamble, staying here," Geer said. "Now you can travel North. No need for papers."

War and the talk of it was all around them clear to understand once he knew what was up.

"Or you can stay and work with me a while."

The choice was his to make. A real choice at last.

Jute's North Star, Canada, fell — a discarded cloak about his feet — starlight of manhood pooled full bloom.

"Yes", he said, their glance a bargain made, a clasp of hands, better than a paper signed between friends. "I'll stay."

'Till I build a mill of my own, he thought.

A promise made to Susu, to himself, to Poppa wherever he was. A promise of peace and growing up free, 'midst shouting talk of war.

*The End.*